*Freedom
for Me
and Other Human
Creatures*

Freedom for Me and Other Human Creatures

Carolyn Keefe

Illustrated by Dennis Bellile

 WORD BOOKS
PUBLISHER
WACO, TEXAS

FREEDOM FOR ME
AND OTHER HUMAN CREATURES

ISBN 0-8499-0037-9
Library of Congress Catalog Card Number: 77-83333
Printed in the United States of America

To my mother
who first taught me about freedom in Christ
and to my husband Fred
who, along with her,
helps me to use it

ACKNOWLEDGMENTS

Grateful acknowledgment is made to the following copyright holders for permission to use their copyrighted material:

Alverno College, for the quotation from the Conference of Women Theologians proceedings transcript.

Cambridge University Press, for the quotation from *Christian Doctrine* by J. S. Whale, 1952.

Charles Scribner's Sons, for quotations from the following: Reinhold Niebuhr, *The Nature and Destiny of Man*, 1953; D. M. Baillie, *God Was in Christ*, 1948.

Concern Magazine, for the article "A Process for Clarifying Values," by Virginia Stieb-Hales.

Eternity Magazine, for the quotation from "Jesus Doesn't Think I'm Dumb" by Nancy B. Barcus, copyright 1974 by Evangelical Ministries, 1716 Spruce St., Philadelphia, PA 19103; for the poem "Rapture" by Carolyn Keefe, copyright 1974 by Evangelical Ministries.

Hawthorn Books, Inc., for quotations from *Whatever Became of Sin?* by Karl Menninger, copyright 1973 by Karl Menninger, M. D.

Harcourt Brace Jovanovich, Inc., for the quotation from *The Four Loves* by C. S. Lewis, © 1960 by Helen Joy Lewis.

HIS, student magazine of Inter-Varsity Christian Fellowship, for the use of "Flowers in the Mine Field" by Barbara J. Sroka, copyright 1974.

John Knox Press, for quotations from the following: C. Ellis Nelson, *Where Faith Begins*, copyright 1967 by M. E. Bratcher; Howard Tillman Kuist, *These Words Upon Thy Heart*, copyright 1947 by John Knox Press; Paul Tournier, *The Meaning of Gifts*, copyright 1963 by M. E. Bratcher.

The Judson Press, for the quotation from Reuel Howe, *Herein Is Love*, copyright 1961, used by permission.

Macmillan Publishing Co., Inc., for the quotation from *Mere Christianity* by C. S. Lewis, copyright 1943, 1945, 1952 by Macmillan Publishing Co., Inc.

Oberlin Alumni Magazine, for the quotation from the Nov.-Dec. 1974 issue.

(Continued on page 8)

6]

CONTENTS

Acknowledgments 6
Preface: From the Shoreline 9
1. The free person faces up to what human beings are like 13
2. The free person is able to make choices 21
3. The free person accepts God's grace 45
4. The free person knows what he values 61
5. The free person accepts responsibility for the outcome of his choices 75
6. The free person has a realistic view of his strengths and weaknesses 89
7. The free person does not fear death 103
Study Guide 119
Bibliography 131

Acknowledgements, continued

Random House, Inc. Alfred A. Knopf, Inc., for quotations from *Male Chauvinism! How It Works* by Michael Korda, copyright 1973; *Markings* by Dag Hammarskjöld, trans. by Leif Sjoberg & W. H. Auden, copyright 1964.

Committee on The Christian Approach to the Jews, for the quotation from "A Letter To Her Mother," *Israel For Christ,* Autumn 1964.

Word Books, Publisher, for quotations from *Conflict and Conscience* by Mark Hatfield, copyright 1971 by Word, Incorporated; *In Search of Balance* by Virginia Mollenkott, copyright 1969 by Word Incorporated.

I would also like to thank the following for permission to use material from conversations, interviews, written statements, and other non-copyrighted material:

Margaret Rogers of Camden, South Carolina, Becky Talley of West Grove, Pennsylvania, and Delena Walker of Kemblesville, Pennsylvania, for their statements on the meaning of God's grace in their lives. Frances A. Eigo, O. S. A., chairman, Department of Religious Studies, Villanova University, for the quotation from his class lectures. Kim Casagrande of Malvern, Pennsylvania, for her drawing on p. 101. Fred Keefe of Upper Darby, Pennsylvania, and Roma Walstrom of Harbor Springs, Michigan, for their quotes. The Reverend Dr. Frederick W. Evans of Cincinnati, Ohio, for his reflections on the death of a friend. Claire Parker of Palm Springs, California, for her letter about the death of her mother. Inter-Varsity Press for permission to reproduce a hymn from their 1947 *Hymns.*

PREFACE

From the Shoreline

Several years ago while I was attending a speech communication convention in Chicago, I decided to go out to see Lake Michigan. So I got up early one morning, buttoned my coat collar high, and set off down Monroe Avenue.

When I started out I was not at all sure what "seeing the lake" would mean. Easily repulsed by severe weather, I had already vowed that if I met the usual wintry blasts on Lake Shore Drive, I would content myself with only a remote glance.

The weather, however, was in my favor, and I found myself drawn through the converging traffic to the very edge of the lake. What pulled me was my own intense desire to experience the lake at close range, to stand where I had not stood for over thirty years, to reclothe my memory with new sights and sounds.

As I walked down the few patched concrete steps which brought me directly to the lake, the shrouded sun was angling at forty-five degrees. The water was fluid but calm with none of the tiny frozen mountains I had known off the winter Michigan shore at Grand Haven. There were no white caps

or blueness, no sand visible through the water, just a strong mounting against the ripples and a great grey expanse toward the horizon. About a hundred yards off shore, a single duck submerged and stayed under so long that I thought it must have succumbed to the cold. Then suddenly up it popped and was immediately joined by a second duck I had not even noticed before. To my left was a lighthouse or two which did not capture my attention for it was fixed elsewhere. On a point to my right, the contours of the Adler Planetarium emerged from the early mist like an almost forgotten fairy tale illustration. Closer in toward shore, the Field Museum of Natural History squared off, solid and substantial. I remembered once visiting there with my mother and being impressed—but it was the stars on the curved ceiling of Adler that had transported me further and more enthrallingly. The years seemed to roll back and yet stand still as I felt myself both a teenager in a lavender print dress and a grown woman snug inside a gray wool midi coat. Mysteriously the lake had become a time machine.

After my youthful memory had been given a middle age booster shot, I turned to face the street sounds which for a quarter hour had come through a layer of dreams. Responsibility awaited me back at the hotel. It was all right for me to return now, for inside myself I knew I had seen the lake.

For me, then, *lake* is not an abstract idea but a series of concrete, sensory experiences of Lake Michigan and many others. Indeed, *lake* is a part of me, a word I react to with pleasure and the impulse to share with others the memory of what I felt when I stood alone on the fringe of Grant Park.

And so it is with *freedom* which is the subject of this book. I see no point in treating the word as a magnificent principle which, along with Love, Beauty, Justice, and Goodness, supposedly exists somewhere—usually just beyond our reach. Instead, I want to talk about freedom as human experience— that of others as well as myself—of freedom as big and little happenings, as how we view ourselves, others, and God. I might say that I want to talk about freedom from the shoreline, not from behind hotel walls.

To do so I shall consider several aspects of freedom which are evident in the lives of the persons I have chosen to believe and follow, and which have been confirmed in my own experience. I shall quote from my mentors—both famous and ordinary—and then do what Benjamin S. Bloom (in *Taxonomy of Educational Objectives,* p. 162*) calls "synthesis," i.e., combining parts of one's previous experience with new material which is then reconstructed into a new and more or less well-integrated whole. The "whole" in this book is not meant to be an exhaustive treatment but to be a very small part of what freedom can mean to all human creatures who look to God as the source of their lives. To say there is more, much more, is to say something about freedom itself. Those who experience it know that they can't circumscribe it. Nor do they want to.

According to educational theorists, synthesizing is a self-expressive activity which represents *"living* at its best and fullest" (Bloom, p. 166). It is for me, and I hope that every reader will likewise engage in a synthesis which will lead him to a new experience of freedom in Jesus Christ.

* Full bibliographical information on all works quoted is given in the bibliography at the end of the book.

1.

The free person faces up to what human beings are like

So God created man in his own image, in the image of God he created him; male and female he created them.

Genesis 1:27

God Is a Midwife

God is a midwife with strong hands
and fingers as long as forceps.
Her wrists can flex a whole turn,
pivot and hold at will,
doing the needful thing to bring birth.
The fetus groans within earth's womb,
begs for yet another day unmolested by sun,
one last curled sleep before the noises start
and meteors devastate the hills.
A midwife cannot give heed to unborn pleas,
for like a mariner crossing a line inked on the sea,
she knows the signs, the starts.
The muscles will prod and pull back,
prod and eject one more child of earth
who still bound to Hades' heart
will feed on folly through cords of twisted clay.
The midwife has seen a billion lyings-in
since Adam's birth. The process repeats,
only the bodies change. Still, she
dare not rest till life is secure
and those who wait turn happily home.

*Consider what it means to be born
human...*

We are "little less than God"

When I look at thy heavens, the work of thy fingers,
    the moon and the stars which thou hast established;
what is man that thou art mindful of him,
    and the son of man that thou dost care for him?
Yet thou hast made him little less than God,
    and dost crown him with glory and honor.
Thou hast given him dominion over the works of thy hands;
    thou hast put all things under his feet,
all sheep and oxen,
    and also the beasts of the field,
the birds of the air, and the fish of the sea,
    whatever passes along the paths of the sea.

                             Psalm 8:3–8

We are "all alike corrupt"

The fool says in his heart, "There is no God."
They are corrupt, they do abominable deeds,
there is none that does good.

The Lord looks down from heaven upon the children of men,
    to see if there are any that act wisely,
    that seek after God.

They have all gone astray, they are all alike corrupt;
    there is none that does good,
    no, not one.

                             Psalm 14:1–3

Do we dare face up to what we see in human beings?

That there are "reasons" behind sin does not correct its offensiveness, its destructiveness, its essential wrongness. If "ignorance of the law excuses no one," ignorance of the truth surely cannot absolve one from all sins of omission. Call it sloth, acedia, apathy, indifference, laziness, callousness, or whatever—if refusal to learn permits the continuance of destructive evil, such willful ignorance is surely wrong.

Some of us can remember in the late thirties how some of our intelligent friends refused to believe what was reported about Hitler's horrible acts and systematic genocide. Granted, the crime was so huge and awful that it staggered the imagination, let alone the credulity of the civilized world. But there were plenty of burning fragments from the great fire thrown into the air for everyone to see and shudder and weep. But many averted their eyes—and ears—striving for a selfish safety which no one could entirely achieve.

KARL MENNINGER, *Whatever Became of Sin?* p. 147

The nature of self-love and of this human Ego is to love self only and consider self only. But what will man do? He cannot prevent this object that he loves from being full of faults and wants. He wants to be great, and he sees himself small. He wants to be happy, and he sees himself miserable. He wants to be perfect, and he sees himself full of imperfections. He wants to be the object of love and esteem among men, and he sees that his faults merit only their hatred and contempt. This embarrassment in which he finds himself produces in him the most unrighteous and criminal passion that can be imagined; for he conceives a mortal enmity against that truth which reproves him and which convinces him of his faults. He would annihilate it, but, unable to destroy it in its essence, he destroys it as far as possible in his own knowledge and in that of others; that is to say, he devotes all his attention to hiding his faults both from others and from himself, and he cannot endure either that others should point them out to him, or that they should see them.

BLAISE PASCAL, *Pensées, II,* 100

The high estimate of the human stature implied in the concept of "image of God" stands in paradoxical juxtaposition to the low estimate of human virtue in Christian thought. Man is a sinner. His sin is defined as rebellion against God. The Christian estimate of human evil is so serious precisely because it places evil at the very centre of human personality: in the will. This evil cannot be regarded complacently as the inevitable consequence of his finiteness or the fruit of his involvement in the contingencies and necessities of nature. Sin is occasioned precisely by the fact that man refuses to admit his "creatureliness" and to acknowledge himself as merely a member of a total unity of life. He pretends to be more than he is. Nor can he, as in both rationalistic and mystic dualism, dismiss his sins as residing in that part of himself which is not his true self, that is, that part of himself which is involved in physical necessity. In Christianity it is not the eternal man who judges the finite man; but the eternal and

[19

holy God who judges sinful man. Nor is redemption in the power of the eternal man who gradually sloughs off finite man. Man is not divided against himself so that the essential man can be extricated from the non-essential. Man contradicts himself within the terms of his true essence. His essence is free self-determination. His sin is the wrong use of his freedom and its consequent destruction.

REINHOLD NIEBUHR
The Nature and Destiny of Man, p. 16

2.

The free person is able to make choices

Some people think they can imagine a creature which was free but had no possibility of going wrong; I cannot. If a thing is free to be good it is also free to be bad. And free will is what has made evil possible. Why, then, did God give them free will? Because free will, though it makes evil possible, is also the only thing that makes possible any love or goodness or joy worth having. A world of automata—of creatures that worked like machines—would hardly be worth creating. The happiness which God designs for His higher creatures is the happiness of being freely, voluntarily united to Him and to each other in an ecstasy of love and delight compared with which the most rapturous love between a man and a woman on this earth is mere milk and water. And for that they must be free.

C. S. Lewis
Mere Christianity, p. 52

We can choose to be delivered from our sin—but often we, like the fetus in this poem, refuse to be new-born.

Choose Dark

She has been pregnant every month
since puberty, filled with a
sprawling, kicking mass
which will not come out.
It shifts beneath her skin
like a golf ball in a rubber glove
and defies her hand to find
the front and back, head and rear.
It intrudes upon her legs
when she brakes the car,
bumps against the wheel
and throws her into skids
which leave stretch marks
on every road she drives.
Adhering her womb is a prankster
who jeers through her veins
and slaps away its last assist
for sunlight and up-drafted bluebirds.

Trust in the Lord with all your heart,
and do not rely on your own insight.
In all your ways acknowledge him,
and he will make straight your paths.

Proverbs 3:5–6

What do these verses have to say about
human choices?

Doesn't God want us to think over
our options carefully?

Really, now—
not use our insight?

Virginia Mollenkott answers:

When I seek to trust in the Lord with all my heart,
and not lean on my own understanding, I must not
repudiate my own insights, nor must I refuse to make
responsible decisions. Instead, I must judge a human
situation as carefully as I can, at the same time remind-
ing myself of my human limitations and the possibility
of my own error. I must pray for God's guidance; I
must consciously open my thoughts to the influence of
the Holy Spirit; I must try to see things as I think God
might see them, all the while aware that I am *not* God
and that ego and self-interest might be skewing my
judgment. As I swing into action, doing the thing which
seems to be right in the situation so far as I can assess it,
I must do so in reliance upon God's guidance and

mercy; but I must not assume my own infallibility. I must perform my deed with a conscious acknowledgment of Him, in confidence that in fulfillment of His promise He will keep me from ultimately devastating error ("he shall direct thy paths"). At the same time, I am protected from a nervous breakdown by the knowledge that God knows my heart, and that I am acting with my trust in Him. If I am wrong in this individual case, He will apply to me the forgiveness made possible by Christ's redemptive death. So I am *simultaneously* resting in God and making responsible human choice.

In Search of Balance, pp. 37–38

Just deciding to seek freedom is not enough—*how* and *where* also matter.

Seeker Lost

I am a twentieth-century Magellan,
a Drake, a Pizarro, or a Cortez,
the girl you saw featured by the Daily News,
the one who set sail to find freedom
and return with it shackled in the hold.
My vessel has touched dock
at every port of seven lands
and waited like a stake-out
while I have boot-clicked through native streets.
I have exhumed stone-cut graves
where freedom should have spilled forth
like buried Yucatan gold.
I have gun-butted bloated priests
whose morning prayers turned manna sour
at noon. I have thrown over boulders
and found slugs, uprooted trees, followed
secret trails, decoyed streams which then mocked me
mapless, a vagabond toting a limp gunnysack.
Freedom has stranded me with no route to the sea.

What about the matter of free will and determinism?

Are we free to make decisions and carry them out or are we at the mercy of forces beyond our control?

This is what some great thinkers have said about the subject:

Man has free choice. Otherwise counsels, exhortations, commands, prohibitions, rewards and punishments would be in vain.

THOMAS AQUINAS, *Summa Theologia,* LXXXIII, 1

For though men may do many things which God does not command, nor is therefore author of them; yet they can have no passion, nor appetite to anything, of which appetite God's will is not the cause. And did not His will assure the necessity of man's will, and consequently of all that on man's will dependeth, the liberty of men would be a contradiction and impediment to the omnipotence and liberty of God.

THOMAS HOBBES, *Leviathan,* XXI

Refuse then to be free, if freedom does not please you; I at least shall rejoice in my liberty, since I experience it in myself, and you have assailed it not with proof but with bare negations merely. Perchance I shall receive more credence from others, because I affirm that which I have experienced and anyone may experience in himself, than you who make your denial merely because you chance not to have experienced it.

RENÉ DESCARTES
Objections Against the Meditations and Replies
Fifth Set, Fourth Med., 3

God alone is a free cause; for God alone exists from the necessity alone of His own nature, and acts from the necessity alone of His own nature.

BARUCH SPINOZA, *Ethics*, I, 17

All theory is against the freedom of the will, all experience for it.

SAMUEL JOHNSON

Each man lives for himself, using his freedom to attain his personal aims, and feels with his whole being that he can now do or abstain from doing this or that action; but as soon as he has done it, that action performed at a certain moment in time becomes irrevocable and belongs to history, in which it has not a free but a predestined significance.

LEO TOLSTOY, *War and Peace*, IX, 1

And now what does the New Testament say? (The italicized sections are my emphasis)

And when [they] heard this [the word of God], they were glad and glorified the word of God; and *as many as were ordained to eternal life believed.* Acts 13:48.

To you therefore who believe, he is precious, but for those who do not believe, "The very stone which the builders rejected has become the head of the corner," and "A stone that will make men stumble, a rock that will

IT'S JUST LIKE I TOLD YOU, SOME PERSONS ARE PREDESTINED TO BELIEVE -- OTHERS ARE NOT.

make them fall"; for they stumble because they disobey the word, *as they were destined to do.* 1 Peter 2:7–8.

YOU'RE WRONG, FRIEND. THE BIBLE CLEARLY TEACHES THAT *EVERY* PERSON IS ABLE TO CHOOSE WHAT HE'LL BELIEVE AND DO!

You search the scriptures, because you think that in them you have eternal life; and it is they that bear witness to me; *yet you refuse to come to me* that you may have life. John 5:39–40.

But I [Paul] preferred to do nothing without your consent in order that your goodness might not be by compulsion but of your own *free will*. Philemon 14.

WAIT A MINUTE, YOU TWO-- HOW ABOUT THE PASSAGES WHICH SHOW **BOTH** SIDES OF THE COIN?

All things have been delivered to me by my Father; and no one knows the Son except the Father, and no one knows the Father except the Son and *any one to whom the Son chooses to reveal him. Come to me,* all who labor and are heavy laden, and I will give you rest. Matthew 11:27–28.

All that the Father gives me will come to me; and *him who comes to me* I will not cast out. John 6:37.

WE'RE CONFUSED-- WHAT SHOULD WE BELIEVE?

Often we say that we "seek the Lord." Is that what really occurs, or has something else taken place? What light does this hymn shed on the question?

I sought the Lord, and afterward I knew

ANON.   GEORGE W. CHADWICK

1 I sought the Lord, and af-ter-ward I knew He moved my
2 Thou didst reach forth Thy hand and mine en-fold; I walked and
3 I find, I walk, I love; but O the whole Of love is

soul to seek Him, seek-ing me; It was not I that
sank not on the storm-vexed sea; 'Twas not so much that
but my an-swer, Lord, to Thee! For Thou wert long be-

found, O Sav-ior true; No, I was found of Thee.
I on Thee took hold, As Thou, dear Lord, on me.
fore-hand with my soul; Al-ways Thou lov-edst me.

Could our seeking and God's finding be part of the same event?

That we are free to choose between options is what makes temptation possible.

If Jesus had not been able to say *yes!* to the Devil in the wilderness, his three *nos* would not have been remarkable.

In this dramatic choral reading, the mother of our Lord is puzzled by three visitors who have come to worship her infant son. Each predicts a great future for him. Mary is torn by her own aspirations for her newborn baby—and for herself.

The Temptation of Mary

A dramatic choral reading using four characters and a six-voice speaking choir

During the entire performance Mary is seated on a low stool, center stage, facing the audience. She is wearing a white flowing garment and she holds a doll wrapped in swaddling clothes. Above her hang a number of mobiles—crosses, crowns, stars, and swords, cut from colored foil which has been glued to both sides of cardboard forms. These shapes dangle from the ceiling on black threads of varying lengths.

The three visitors are draped in flowing material such as sheeting or cheesecloth which has been dyed a vivid hue. Visitor I's garment is cerise, Visitor II's is purple, and Visitor III's is deep red.

Five members of the choral speaking group wear black or maroon choir robes. Voice 4 is attired in a white robe. The speakers stand in two rows of three, to the left and backstage from Mary.

The lament of the daughters of Jerusalem can be pretaped and used at the appropriate place in the play. Careful timing is required to synchronize the action and the wailing, but the effectiveness of the dramatization is heightened by this method. If no tape recorder is available, several women off-stage or hidden by a screen can do the wailing.

Mary: (Hums lullaby, then speaks) Now hush, my babe. The nine long months are over, the time when the sweet essence of heaven wrought within me that of which I did not know.

But here now is flesh and blood, hair and skin—and eyes which gaze at me with sight which goes beyond their few brief hours of life.

For me it is all too strange and wonderful. Mere pondering cannot reveal the mystery—or else would I not know from whence you came, and how, and why? And in the knowing perhaps I would cease my endless questioning—and the doubts and fears would fly away this day with the first light of dawn.

But now it is enough to have this miracle incarnate in my arms, to share my joy with the whole universe in this glad hour.

Voice 1:   The morning stars sang together and all the sons of God shouted for joy.

Voice 2:   My heart and flesh sing for joy to the living God. Glory to God in the highest!

Voices 1 and 2:   Sing praises to God, sing praises!
          Sing praises to our King, sing praises!

Voice 3:   Make a joyful noise to the Lord, all the earth.

Voices 3, 5, and 6:   Let the sea roar.

Voice 5:   Let the floods clap their hands.

Voice 2:   Let the hills sing for joy.

Voices 1, 2, and 3:   Sing praises to God, sing praises!

Voice 1:   My soul magnifies the Lord and my spirit rejoices in God my Savior. Glory to God in the highest!

Voice 4:   These things have I spoken to you that my joy may be in you and that your joy may be full.

All: Sing praises to God, sing praises!
     Sing praises to our King, sing praises!

Mary: (Startled) Hark! Who comes here? Another sent from God?

(Visitor I enters from stage right and kneels before Mary)

Visitor I: Hail Thou Supplier of Israel, in Thee do I place my hope! How small are your baby hands, yet someday they will break the loaves which will revive our bodies long weakened by hunger. Then eager feet will again run to the once dry stream beds, now swollen by the early rains, and there stop in wonderment. The famine is past, not for a time as fixed by seasons or conquerors.

(Visitor rises to his/her feet and stands at an angle to the right of Mary. His/her tone is reminiscent.)

It was not always thus. There was a day when hunger sat upon the walls of Samaria. It watched while a city, diminishing by degrees, slaughtered hope in the doing. Outside camped Syria, fat and secure waiting for what they knew would surely be the victorious end, not by assault but by time. Then came the prophetic word to ears rendered dull by lack—"Tomorrow about this time a measure of fine meal shall be sold for a shekel at the gate of Samaria." *(Sarcastically)* Fine delusion evoked from the memories of a grander day!

But then, there it was spread out before us—heaped in the plains, massed in the forsaken tents now left silent by the detestable enemy, Food! More than just enough of it!

(Triumphantly)

So from this sacred place issue forth Thou Feeder of the flock of Israel. We hail Thee as Lord, Thou who art above the kings of the earth. Thou art the King of Heaven! *(In a calculating manner)* We care not whose image is borne on the copper coin. Nebuchadnezzar, Cyrus, Darius? At least they fed us.

Voice 4: Man shall not live by bread alone.

Voice 5: Jesus then took the loaves, and when He had given thanks, He distributed them to those who were seated, so also the fish, as much as they wanted.

Voices 1 and 3: Perceiving then that they were about to come and take Him by force to make Him king, Jesus withdrew again to the hills by Himself.

Voice 4: I am the bread of life; he who comes to me shall not hunger, and he who believes in me shall never thirst.

(Pause)

Take eat, this is my body.

Voices 1, 2, 3, 5, and 6: Give us this day our daily bread.

Voice 4: Man shall not live by bread alone but by every word that proceeds from the mouth of God.

(Visitor II enters from stage right and kneels before Mary.)

Visitor II: Hail Thou Son of David, King of Israel! In Thee do I place my hope! How small are your baby hands, yet some day they shall hold the sceptre of David and on your head will the high priest place the diadem of gold.

(He/she rises and stands to the right of Visitor I.)

How the starlight gathers together in one place, forming a luminous crown for your head. So should it be, fair babe. A man ruddy and handsome, beautiful of eyes was your father David. No mortal since has known such grace, such a command of voice, such presence. He was authority, enfleshed; thus shall you be, leading and directing the fortunes of our people, uniting the long-lost house of Jacob into a nation ruled by God's own choice. Then the eyes of conquerors and the conquered will focus on a Jew. The shaking of heads and the hissing will cease. "Long live King Jesus," they will shout as you sweep into the city where now we cower before our oppressors. What then of favors to Herod, of the bowing and the falling, of the saying "Yes" with our forced smiles?

(Rousing manner) Rise up now, O babe of Bethlehem, the root and offspring of David. Go forth to lead Thy people into the Kingdom of God!

Voice 4: *(In a strong voice)* Repent for the Kingdom of heaven is at hand. The Kingdom of God is in the midst of you.

All: Thy Kingdom come, Thy will be done on earth as it is in heaven.

Voices 1, 2, and 3: Tell the Daughter of Zion—

Voices 5 and 6: Behold your King is coming to you

Voice 6:   Humble and mounted on an ass

Voice 5:   And on a colt, the foal of an ass.

Voices 1, 2, 3, and 6:   But seek ye first His Kingdom and His righteousness.

Voice 4:   My Kingdom is not of this world.

Not everyone who says to me,

Voices 1, 2 and 3:   "Lord, Lord,"

Voice 4:   Shall enter the Kingdom of Heaven, but he who does the will of my Father who is in heaven.

All: Our Father who art in Heaven—Thy Kingdom come.

(Visitor III enters and kneels before Mary.)

Visitor III: Hail Thou Warrior of Israel! In Thee do I place my hope. How small are your baby hands, yet some-day they will brandish the devouring sword and your lips will shout the cry to battle.

(He/she rises and stands to the right of Visitor II.)

There lay our golden warriors, slain by the hordes from beyond the River. The seige was not over in a day, nor a month, nor a year. *(Disgusted)* Why could not Jeremiah be hushed, he with his babblings and twitterings about the doom of God's people? The whole land become a ruin and a waste? Not the city of David upon which God had uttered His word of blessing, not the land called Promised which was given to our fathers as an eternal inheritance! But still they came, leaping, battering, slaughtering, plundering with their accursed Marduk mounted on their spears. "See now," they derided us, "our gods have led us through the shimmering River, over your mountains of defense and your tower-topped walls to a people who no longer shall be called a people but slaves."

But stay not long, small babe, in the shelter of your mother's arms. *(Flourishing manner)* Go forth, brave heart, to conquer, to avenge, to vindicate Thy people. "Let them vanish like water that runs away; like grass let them be trodden down and wither."

Voice 4:   But I will have pity on the house of Judah, and I will deliver them by the Lord their God; I will not deliver them—

Voice 1: by the bow

Voice 2: by the sword

Voices 1, 2, and 3: nor by war

Voice 5: nor by horses

Voices 5 and 6: nor by horsemen.

All: All who take the sword will perish by the sword.

Voice 3: For out of Zion shall go forth the law, and the word of the Lord from Jerusalem.

Voice 5: He shall judge between the nations, and shall decide for many peoples;

Voice 1: And they shall beat their swords into plowshares

Voice 2: And their spears into pruning hooks.

Voice 6: Nation shall not lift up sword against nation.

Voices 1, 2, and 6: Neither shall they learn war any more.

Voice 4: If my Kingship were of this world, my servants would fight.

Voices 1 and 2: "Not by might

Voices 5 and 6: nor by power

Voice 3: But by my spirit," says the Lord of hosts.

Voice 1: Glory to God in the highest, and on earth peace.

(During this succession of visitors Mary's emotions have ranged from joy to wonderment. She has listened intently to the three Visitors and has attended to the words of the choir. Now she is puzzled by conflicting ideas and aspirations.)

Mary: What manner of child is this to be worshiped and commissioned by three such strange visitors! How their words do speak forth the desires of my own heart. A provider? A ruler? A conqueror? Did not the angel assign to Him the throne of His father David?

(Pause)

Yet Gabriel spoke the word "You will call His name Jesus for He will save His people from their sins."

(Questioningly) Savior? *(Affirmatively)* Savior.
(Low mourning begins, quietly, then gradually becomes louder.)

O joyful heart, listen to the wailings in the night. Soft women's voices, mourning as for one whose right it was to walk the earth, cries from a mother whose son has been called from the land of all that is to enter that vale of which we know not.

(Pause)

The voices are not unlike those which I know, tunes which speak to me of friend, of kin.

(Pause. Then she reassures herself.)

But no, it cannot be. The stillness of the night must call to my ears sounds from some unreal world of dreams.

Yet there rises the cry of the daughters of Jerusalem whose eyes have looked on death, whose mouths, unable to form words, utter only groans of pain for which there is no balm on earth.

Can it be that the ecstasy of this night is to be snatched from me by the thought of the morrow, by the knowledge that there will come growth, then the seeking out of His own path? But I must not stunt this! He must find His own way in His world, He must be free to catch the rays of the sun in His hand—to give them to whom He will, to meet God where I cannot follow Him.

(Desperately)

Oh, but will that wailing never cease? For I hear the cries of my own heart mingled with those of my friends.

(The next section is read slowly and gravely, backgrounded by laments.)

Voice 6: He was despised and rejected by men; a man of sorrows and acquainted with grief.

Voice 4: But I am a worm and no man; scorned by men and despised by the people. All who see me mock me, they wag their heads.

[41

Voice 3:   He was oppressed and He was afflicted.

Voices 1 and 5:   Yet He opened not His mouth;

Voice 2:   Like a lamb that is led to the slaughter

Voice 6:   And like a sheep that before his shearers is dumb

Voices 2 and 6:   So He opened not His mouth.

Mary: *(Defiantly)* Cannot the joy of this night speak "no" to the One who heralds that my son will choose to walk the path of thorns? Such is not to be—not my son whose visage bears the image of strength, of nobility—like that of God Himself. No weakling He! Not his the lot to be buffeted and mocked, scoffed and rejected. His life must not be like that of the red anemone blasted in a single hour by the bold sirocco.

> *(Here wailing fades out in a low drone, blending into the faint strains of "Worthy Is the Lamb" from Handel's* Messiah.)

Voices 1 and 3:   Surely He hath borne our griefs and carried our sorrows. He was wounded for our transgressions, He was bruised for our iniquities; upon Him was the chastisement that made us whole, and with His stripes we are healed.

Voice 5:   Yet it was the will of the Lord to bruise Him; He has put Him to grief.

Voice 1:   When He makes Himself an offering for sin, He shall see His offspring.

Voice 3:   He shall prolong His days.

Voices 1 and 3:   The will of the Lord shall prosper in His hand.

Voice 2:   He shall see the fruit of the travail of His soul and be satisfied.

Voices 1, 2, and 3:   By His knowledge shall the righteous one, my servant, make many to be accounted righteous.

Voice 5:   He shall bear their iniquities.

All: Glory to God in the highest and on earth peace among men with whom He is pleased.

Mary: *(Quietly but resolutely)* First came the pain, slowly, unlike any that I had felt before, and then the sharpness rose casting me into a world inhabited by the shades of Death, but there too dwelt Hope. And God moved among the shadows.

(*Triumphantly*) Then the babe did cry—such an omen of days to come! But with that sound came joy unspeakable which even now has begun to dim the memory of travail. Blessed relief, though not just a surcease from pain, but a filling of the void with the enfolding presence of God, infusing all these hours with moment—incomprehensible, sweet, sad, still triumphant. It is finished—yet only begun. Such is the glory of this night of stars and of voices from the past and the future.

Voice 4:   I am the bread of life.

(Pause)

I am the root and offspring of David.

(Pause)

I am a sharp two-edged sword.

(Pause)

I am the Savior of the world.

Voice 1:   Though He was in the form of God, Jesus Christ did not count equality with God a thing to be grasped.

Voice 5:   He humbled Himself

Voice 3:   And became obedient unto death

Voices 3 and 5:   Even death on a cross.

All: Therefore God has highly exalted Him

Voice 2:   And bestowed on Him

Voices 1, 3, 5, and 6:   THE NAME THAT IS ABOVE EVERY NAME.

All·   That at the name of Jesus every knee should bow

Voice 1:   in heaven

Voice 2:   and on earth

Voice 6:   and under the earth

All: and every tongue confess that Jesus Christ is Lord, to the glory of God the Father.

Voice 4:   AMEN.

[43

All: AMEN.

(The music grows louder and plays through to end of first part of selection: "Blessing and honor and glory and power be unto Him, forever," etc. The long Amen which follows should be deleted.)

3.
The free person accepts God's grace

Where sin increased, grace abounded all the more.
Romans 5:20 b

As grace is first from God,
so it is continually from him,
as much as light is all day long from the sun,
as well as at first dawn or at sun-rising.
JONATHAN EDWARDS

May it not be a persistent relic of the self-centredness which is the essence of sin, and even of the pride which is its most deadly form, because it will not accept the forgiveness of sins; the pride that makes us refuse "justification by faith" and choose "justification by works"? The Christian way is the very opposite. It sets us free for the service of God and man by delivering us from ourselves. And so its ultimate confession . . . is: Not I, but the grace of God.

D. M. BAILLIE, *God Was in Christ,* pp. 169–70

There is no one way to respond to God's grace in Jesus Christ

Some remember exactly when it happened—others don't.

A person may weep—or laugh—or shout—or just be silent.

For some it is an intense emotional experience, for others a long developing realization that Jesus Christ is Lord indeed!

Dag Hammarskjöld

Whitsunday, 1961

I don't know Who—or what—put the question, I don't know when it was put. I don't even remember answering. But at some moment I did answer *Yes* to Someone—or Something—and from that hour I was certain that existence is meaningful and that, therefore, my life, in self-surrender, had a goal.

From that moment I have known what it means "not to look back," and "to take no thought for the morrow."

Led by the Ariadne's thread of my answer through the labyrinth of Life, I came to a time and place where I realized that the Way leads to a triumph which is a catastrophe, and to a catastrophe which is a triumph, that the price for commiting one's life would be reproach, and that the only elevation possible to man lies in the depths of humiliation. After that, the word "courage" lost its meaning, since nothing could be taken from me.

[49

As I continued along the Way, I learned, step by step, word by word, that behind every saying in the Gospels stands *one* man and *one* man's experience. Also behind the prayer that the cup might pass from him and his promise to drink it. Also behind each of the words from the Cross.

Markings, p. 205

Charles G. Finney

There was no fire, and no light, in the room; nevertheless it appeared to me as if it were perfectly light. As I went in and shut the door after me, it seemed as if I met the Lord Jesus Christ face to face. It did not occur to me then, nor did it for some time afterward, that it was wholly a mental state. On the contrary it seemed to me that I saw him as I would see any other man. He said nothing, but looked at me in such a manner as to break me right down at his feet. I have always since regarded this as a most remarkable state of mind; for it seemed to me a reality, that he stood before me, and I fell down at his feet and poured out my soul to him. I wept aloud like a child, and made such confessions as I could with my choked utterance. It seemed to me that I bathed his feet with my tears; and yet I had no distinct impression that I touched him, that I recollect.

. . . .

No words can express the wonderful love that was shed abroad in my heart. I wept aloud with joy and love; and I do not know but I should say, I literally bellowed out the unutterable gushings of my heart. These waves came over me, and over me, and over me, one after the other, until I recollect I cried out, "I shall die if these waves continue to pass over me." I said, "Lord, I cannot bear any more"; yet I had no fear of death.

How long I continued in this state, with this baptism continuing to roll over me and go through me, I do not know. But I know it was late in the evening when a member of my choir—for I was the leader of the choir—came into my office to see me. He was a member of the church. He found me in this state of loud weeping, and said to me, "Mr. Finney, what ails you?" I could make him no answer for some time. He then said, "Are you in pain?" I gathered myself up as best I could, and replied, "No, but so happy that I cannot live."

Memoirs, pp. 19–21

Mark Hatfield

It took me a long time to discover the difference [between a religion of habit and a religion of commitment]. But I remember vividly the night in 1954 when it all came to a head. I was sitting alone in my room in my parents' home. For months my words in the classroom had been coming back to mock me. I was urging my students to stand up and be counted, but I was a very silent and very comfortable Christian. That night in the quiet of my room the choice was suddenly made clear. I could not continue to drift along as I had been doing, going to church because I had always gone, because everyone else went, because there wasn't any particular reason not to go. Either Christ was God and Savior and Lord or he wasn't; and if he were, then he had to have all my time, all my devotion, all my life.

I made the choice that night, many years ago; I *committed* myself to Christ. I saw that for thirty-one years I had lived for self, and I decided I wanted to live the rest of my life for Jesus Christ. I asked God to forgive my self-centeredness and to make me his own. I was assured by the words of Paul, "Therefore if any man be in Christ, he is a new creature: old things are passed away; behold, all things are become new" (2 Cor. 5:17).

Conflict and Conscience, p. 98

C. S. Lewis

The things I assert most vigorously are those that I resisted long and accepted late.

. . . .

I know very well when, but hardly how, the final step was taken. I was driven to Whipsnade one sunny morning. When we set out I did not believe that Jesus Christ is the Son of God, and when we reached the zoo I did.

Surprised by Joy, pp. 213, 237

In writing to her mother, a completed Jewess describes her new life in Christ:

It is not sentimentalism, it is not weak; it is strong. It is not an escape from life, nor yet a way of making the unpleasant moments of life more bearable; it is not a bed of roses, nor yet an easy solution to happiness; it is simply a way of being alive that no non-Christian can understand. It means I am alive now in Him and will be forever.

"A Letter to Her Mother"

Three twentieth-century women talk about the meaning of grace in their lives

Margaret Rogers Grace is God's gift to us of forgiveness and acceptance even though we have done nothing to be worthy of this gift. All we have to do is *really* believe. God loves us so much that he gave his Son that this forgiveness could be possible.

My problem is when I do good works because I love God and believe that it is his will that I do these things, I begin to feel that I'm good because of what I do. I believe that we need to be constantly reminded that we could never do enough good works to outweigh the sins we have done against God. So without grace we'd be forever trying to do the impossible. This does not mean we should not do anything, but our good works are a result of God working through us.

<hr />

Becky Talley After we get to the place where we admit we need help, that we cannot save ourselves by ourselves, we can turn to God for forgiveness and accept his gift of salvation through Jesus Christ. When we accept this gift, we are accepting God to lead our everyday living, admitting that we cannot do it by ourselves. It is then that his Holy Spirit helps us perform "the good works which God prepared beforehand," as Paul says.

We do not even think up the good works we must do. They are prepared by God to be presented to us after we accept Jesus Christ. By then we are able to recognize these opportunities as God's will. Before we probably didn't see

[53

them or weren't interested—or if we did attempt good works, it was to impress our friends and neighbors and perhaps to impress God.

After accepting the gift of God's grace, we have the Holy Spirit to help us carry on God's work in this world, not for reward, because that was given before we started, but because our purpose is now to work for God and not for ourselves. Things will still go wrong and we will make mistakes, but God will forgive. He never promised to make us perfect but promised in spite of our great imperfection, salvation through Jesus Christ.

•●··●··●··●··●··●··●··●··●··●··●··●··●··●·

Delena Walker   Grace is the almost unbelievable gift from God by which he accepts me as I am, *sin and all*. Truly this shows me his great love for me and other Christians. To know that for salvation I have only to believe in God and the rest will follow is overwhelming. Sadly enough it seems beyond the comprehension of too many people.

Once you have obtained grace, your entire life begins to change. From my own experience, I can see where my thinking about myself, my own personal problems, and the people around me have undergone a change which I feel has come about only because of my new insights. It's as if I see things in a new perspective now.

Works are, of course, important also, but only as they are prompted by grace. Putting works before grace is like putting the cart before the horse. What a difference there is in doing something for the glory of God instead of for the glory of the individual!

I thank God often that he has led me to a church where grace is uppermost and not works. It's as if a great weight has been lifted from my shoulders, and I finally feel that I've found my niche. Before it seemed to take up so much time performing the various works that I never could get around to really worshiping God and learning more about him and the Bible. Now I can concentrate solely on learning more about the triune God and his teachings. Now I feel that I'm on the right road at last, even though I'll always be just on the way.

Just one other thing—it's as if now I can let the barriers down. Before the barriers were always there, and now I don't see them as often. A direct outcome of grace, I think.

"Grace is a gift from God"

"Grace is a gift from God." This metaphor, two thousand years old, yet still leaping from the New Testament, is confirmed by experience. Three women have just said so, and now a famous Swiss physician shows grace-as-gift has a present and a future meaning.

The great gift, the unique and living one, is not a thing but a person. It is Jesus Christ himself. In him God has given himself, no longer just things which he creates or has created, but his own person, his own suffering, and his own solitude, given unto death itself. He declared it himself, just before turning to face his cross, "Greater love has no man than this, that a man lay down his life for his friend." This gift of all gifts is the self-commitment of God himself, who carried it through to the bitter end so that we may entrust ourselves to it.

The almost unbelievable news of the revelation is that it really is a gift. It is free, without reservation and without recall. Whatever our virtues may be, whatever may be our times of repentance, they all would be unequal to the payment of such a treasure. Thus it is that God offers it freely. He is the One who has paid its price, in the death of his Son. The erasure of all our failings and all our remorse, of all our regrets and our rebellion, what a gift it is! The redemption of all our joys about to be swallowed up in death, and their fulfillment in eternal joy itself—what a gift indeed!

The gift does not end at death, for Christ went beyond the cross—he rose from the dead; he is seated on God's right hand; he shall come. He told us that he will gather men from the four corners of the earth so that they may partake of his glory even as he has partaken of their sufferings. Then it is that all suffering, frustration, and humiliation will have found meaning: participation in the imperishable fellowship of God who himself has suffered in order to present it to us as a gift.

PAUL TOURNIER, *The Meaning of Gifts,* pp. 61–62

This poem shows another way of looking at God's grace.

The Cross Is a Magnet

A child knows the mysterious metal
where fairies play and stretch out tiny wands
which push and pull the world in place.
Magnets are soldiers snapped against the stove,
plastic-skin mummies infused with jumping bean life,
engines towing ten tons of bricks
from foundry to the fort.
Big and small and horseshoe shaped,
ladybugs and frogs and kissing dolls,
Scotty dogs, one black, one white,
cavort toward poles, and lo,
join North and South.

A giant magnet hungry for ore
sweeps over my life and probes my languid land.
It swings, scans, seeks, returns,
orderly motion servant to task,
a dropping arc above my secret fault,
the pendulous pull from God's own cross.
The hoarding rock stirs restlessly below,
its grounded voice shuddering the word:
"Behold, Someone greater has come. Let all
the earth lie open before Him."
My deep, imbedded, undisturbed sin,
now anxious for the lifting,
gives way to attraction.
The molecules scramble, take position.
Then it-is-finished silence
covers me with childlike wonder.

When a person trusts Jesus Christ as his Savior, he experiences *freedom* as *choice* and *grace*. This account took place during the fourth century, but if the language were updated, thousands of today's Christians could say: "That's how I felt when I gave my life to Jesus."

And this Thy whole gift was, to nill what I willed, and to will what Thou willedst. But where through all those years, and out of what low and deep recess was my free-will called forth in a moment, whereby to submit my neck to Thy "easy yoke," and my shoulders unto Thy "light burthen," O Christ Jesus, "my Helper and my Redeemer"? How sweet did it at once become to me to want the sweetnesses of those toys! and what I feared to be parted from was now a joy to part with. For Thou didst cast them forth from me, Thou true and highest sweetness. Thou castest them forth, and for them enteredst in Thyself, sweeter than all pleasure, though not to flesh and blood; brighter than all light, but more hidden than all depths; higher than all honour, but not to the high in their own conceits. Now was my soul free from the biting cares of canvassing and getting, and weltering in filth, and scratching off the itch of lust. And my infant tongue spake freely to Thee, my brightness, and my riches, and my health, the Lord my God.

SAINT AUGUSTINE, *Confessions*, IX, I, 1

One can only learn about life as one
learns about God. A relationship with
God, as revealed in Jesus Christ, is the
highest relationship which man can
achieve.

MARK HATFIELD, *Conflict and
Conscience,* p. 99

4.

The free person knows what he values

Do not lay up for yourselves treasures on earth, where moth and rust consume and where thieves break in and steal, but lay up for yourselves treasures in heaven, where neither moth nor rust consumes and where thieves do not break in and steal. For where your treasure is, there will your heart be also.

Matthew 6:19–21

Where your treasure is

"Values clarification" is the modern term for examining one's personal values. A value is a conceptualization of how we feel about the desirability of some belief or action. When translated into words, a value might come out as, "Yes, I think a national health plan would be a good thing" or "The school board should buy some new buses." The words *good* and *should* are not random choices; they indicate that our feelings about a given matter have moral implications. By their very nature, values have to do with worth—how we perceive right and wrong, good and bad, desirable and undesirable, advantageous and disadvantageous. "People feel that in any situation," says G. Ellis Nelson in *Where Faith Begins,* "there is a way one should act, and they either express themselves in the light of their values or they talk about the situation to find, in the company of others in the same situation, what the values should be" (p. 50). Even when not expressed audibly, our values open up possibilities for action—shall I buy the economy car or the gas-eater?—and we make choices we can live with, or otherwise we distort our perceptions in order to convince ourselves that we indeed have done the desirable, the good thing.

Putting a finger on our values is not as easy as it sounds. Many concepts which we think are values are only weak personal preferences. Theorists say that if an individual has a genuine value, he will be willing, even eager, to put it into effect. Consider this negative example. The mother of two primary age children is adamant: "Certainly, I don't believe that violence on TV is good for my youngsters. But now I'm busy in my garden and can't go inside to shut off the set. Tomorrow I won't let them see 'Crime City.' " And when tomorrow comes, she's talking on the phone while three murders and a robbery are dramatized for the viewers. What the mother *says* she values is not acted upon; yet she'd probably still insist, "Oh, but I do care more for my children than gardening or gossiping." Her arranging of priorities indicates what she *really* values. Our Lord's words cut right across one hundred generations: "For where your treasure is, there will your heart be also."

Taking a look at our values is in itself a value. Long ago Socrates observed that the unexamined life is not worth living. Jesus himself taught that how we respond to the possibilities offered by life should be scrutinized carefully. Ways and means should be considered; one path should be compared to another; and choices leading to a God-filled life should be followed. But always the process should be alert and enlightened. Christ had plenty to say about the five lovely ladies who were so muddled that they missed the biggest social event of the season, indeed of history.

While the virgins' behavior was foolish, it was not unusual. An experiment done at Harvard University determined how adolescents made decisions. Results showed that 18 percent acted impulsively, 18 percent intuitively, 17 percent compliantly, 10 percent fatalistically, and 12 percent paralytically (unable to make choices). Only 25 percent used planning as the basis for deciding.

If these statistics hold true for adolescents in general, and if planning is superior to any other approach to decision making, then parents should diligently and early teach their children what values are and how they lead to action. Then maybe we'd eliminate some of the hypocrisies of life, such as the supposed value one dear lady told me about: "My John and Sammy just love your husband's preaching." I smiled back, glad to hear that my husband had hit two marks. On second thought I wondered why her John and Sammy almost never came to church. Either the mother or her sons were conjuring up values which like magic rabbits were nothing more than mental or manual illusions.

On my first job I discovered how values lead to action, although at the time I could not have verbalized about it. Before I turned sixteen I clerked at a downtown ladies apparel shop. My friend Phyllis Smith had put in a good word for me, and I in turn had piggybacked some of my high school friends until eventually the whole floor was staffed by rather close associates. We weren't a bad bunch, quite conscientious, I'd say, addicted to clothes, not boy-crazy but giggly and loquacious. Our floor manager, Miss Stanzak, was an austere, man-suited female who wore her hair swept up all around into a high pompadour. To us she was the epitome of business—all business, all the time. Even now her favorite directives ring loud and clear: "All right, girls, don't lean on the cases." "That's it, girls, straighten up the stock. The cardigans are out of line." "That's enough kibitzing, girls. Mind the customers."

In between our chatter about clothes, teachers, and boys, we'd discuss how hard we worked and how little we were paid. The women on the wartime factory assembly lines were raking it in, and there we were struggling along with hardly enough to pay for our sloppy Joe sweaters. It just wasn't fair. Why the way we worked for "Stan" should merit us a nice pay boost!

Gradually a bold strategy emerged from our informal labor meetings. We would go on strike for higher wages. The most opportune time would be a Saturday morning before a Monday holiday. Customers would be flocking to buy shorts, slacks, and bathing suits, and unless Stan gave us a raise, there's be no one to "mind the customers."

I can still see the shock on Stan's face as she briskly swung around the corner and discovered all her "girls" standing behind the exterior window display. "What's this, girls?" she demanded.

As one of the chief provocateurs, I replied, "We're not going to work today."

"And why not?" she asked, more flustered than we had ever seen her.

"Well—we think we're underpaid," chimed in another ringleader.

"Come in, come in, girls. You get to work and we'll talk about it later."

Not easily put off, we stood firm. Before we straightened out one blouse or punched one register key, we had negotiated a modest raise.

So we had one up on Stan, but the victory wasn't nearly as sweet as I had expected it would be. Quite obviously we had insulted our boss, even defied her in a brash manner. Without privately consulting her about our grievances, we had chosen an extreme measure which reflected back on each of us. The interpersonal relations between management and labor grew increasingly strained. We made a bit more money but had a lot less fun.

Eventually I felt that I should look elsewhere for a job. I landed in a drugstore where almost immediately I was given heavy responsibilities which satisfied my ego and pushed aside unpleasant thoughts about the "wildcat" strike.

As I look back on this experience, I can see how we girls enacted our value: we did something about what we believed were unfair wages. In so doing we turned our backs upon more moderate and fair approaches to the problem. Possibly we could have attained our goal without hurting another human being, perhaps not. But by confronting Stan on that early Saturday morning, we set in motion a series of events and reactions which we shaped and which shaped us. We had chosen between values, an action which no other member of God's earthly creation could have done.

As for myself, I was well on my way to understanding how values are related to choice and choice to responsibility and responsibility to freedom.

A Process for Clarifying Values

by Virginia Stieb-Hales

How does one know how to guide one's life through a world full of confusion and conflict? We used to live in a homogenous environment, it seems, with obvious and constantly reinforced values. But today we live in a pluralistic society. We live in a world "bombarded on all sides by many points of view, and we are brought in contact daily with other people who have different life styles from our own." We live in a world of contradictions, growing uncertainties, complexity and change. Decisions and choices press upon us constantly. More and more *life* questions are demanding to be answered.

How do we find out what is important to us? How do we answer such questions as, "What am I doing with my life? my time? my strength?" Answering these questions is related to the process of *valuing*.

"People who have not clarified for themselves what they value cannot have clear, consistent purposes, cannot know what they are for and against, cannot know where they are going and why. They lack criteria for choosing what to do with their time, their energy, their very being. Given the complexities of our time, given the staggering number of choices to be made, given the crying need of individuals and

Condensed and reprinted from *Concern*, July-August 1973, by permission.

systems for a direction toward which to move, is there anything we can do to help each other build a value system by which to live?"

It seems that one of the reasons the church has been unable to tackle the issues of our day with a sense of commitment is that we do not know what our values are any more. We need to find out what issues are important to us and then decide on the steps we can take to work on these issues.

What we do is what we value but do we know it is our value? There may be a gap between what we say is important and what we do about it. That gap in itself makes a statement about us and what we value. Do you examine what you do by reflecting on your values? Are you acting on *your* values or values handed to you by the culture? When you buy a house in a community, for instance, have you examined the values of that community? When you move into a community, you are also agreeing to a set of values. Are they *your* values?

What sorts of things are really meaningful to us? What are we striving for and working toward? What sort of a world do we want to see come into being? A value represents something that is important in life.

"The first step in the value clarification process is to open up the area of concern, to stimulate a person to think about value-related issues and to share those thoughts."

The second step is for the person and those around her to accept her thoughts or feelings, nonjudgmentally. This step tells her that it is safe to be honest with herself and others.

The third step is to stimulate the person to do some additional thinking so that she moves toward a more comprehensive level of valuing.

In our traditional teaching, we have thought we could give values or a value system to another person. Some of the traditional approaches to values have been efforts to persuade and convince others by presenting arguments and reasons for this or that set of values, or making rules and regulations intended to contain and mold behavior until it is unthinkingly accepted as "right," or presenting cultural and religious dogma as unquestioned wisdom and truth. Strong emotional appeals to the conscience is another way of trying to enforce values. "Our people have always done it this way," appeals to custom or tradition. These procedures of the past fail to help people grapple with the confusion and conflict that abound in these baffling days.

In place of indoctrination there are some guidelines to a process of valuing that can help people to choose their own values, to close the gap between what they say is important to them and what they do about it in their lives. The process of valuing can help give a sense of direction in a world of contradictions.

The required climate for values clarification is one of genuine respect and acceptance (but not permissiveness or manipulation). We cannot help others to think critically on value-related issues when we demand, however subtly, that the outcome of their thinking conform to what we believe. To help persons clarify their values, do not ask questions that demand a yes-no or an either-or answer. Such answers limit thinking. Also, instead of asking "why" to another's statement of belief or value judgment, ask, "Do you have a reason?"

The following are the seven criteria worked out by one group for discovering one's values. A value should meet *all* seven criteria.

Choosing

1. Choosing freely. Values must be freely selected if they are to be really valued by an individual.

2. Choosing from among alternatives. Only when there is more than one possibility from which to choose, can a value result.

3. Choosing after thoughtful consideration of the alterna-

tives. This is a process of accepting some things, rejecting others.

Prizing

4. Prizing and cherishing. Values are prized, respected and held dear; they come from choices we are glad to make.

5. Affirming. When we have chosen something freely, after consideration of the alternatives, and when we are proud of our choice, we are likely to affirm that choice.

Acting

6. Acting upon choices. Where we have a value, we are likely to budget time and energy in ways that nourish this value.

7. Repeating. Values tend to have a persistence; they tend to make a pattern in life.

The values process asks many "you" questions and insists that the person confront issues suggested by the content. These issues should involve her in choices that are relevant to her day-to-day life.

With change taking place so rapidly and new issues continually requiring consideration, all of us need to reexamine our purposes, aspirations, attitudes and feelings if we are to strive toward a life that will be rich and full for ourselves and others in the times in which we live.

Note: Louis Raths, Merrill Harmin, and Sidney B. Simon, *Values and Teaching* (Columbus, OH: Charles E. Merrill, 1966) and Howard Kirschenbaum, "A World of Confusion and Conflict," *Penney's Forum* (Spring/Summer 1972), have been the basic source of quotations and concepts in presenting this interpretation of the values clarification process.

There are some ways of living that seem to have more value than others. At least, that is the opinion of the old woman in this poem.

A Quality of Dreams

The old live on memories, you say,
a tapestry hung full length
through a hall dank with the smell
of crepy flesh, a panorama
for the walkway from the shadows
to the dark, the mottled mold
of a thousand schemes gone wrong
but revered as though a Tabard
had woven colors into forms
and pronounced them beautiful.

I do not expect you to believe
that once I owned a pure white unicorn
and a prince to go with it,
a castle too with ten golden spires
which reached straight into the sky.
Sometimes the clouds would come down
and be a ship or a place to hide,
a ski slope in summer, a haystack in spring.
Memories are made of the stuff of dreams
and dreams are clouds and clouds
are wind pictures, the artist's wash
where one day I saw my unicorn of old
stabbed dead between his eyes
and my prince—my prince wore tattered robes
and had a tired face.

Tomorrow I may romp in cornfields

staked high with the leftover smiles of summer.
All will be light and warm there
and autumn's late sun will chase me among
the shocks until panting *I* shall fall and sleep,
far from your dreary hall, my friend,
where unicorns never lived and died.

Since men's loyalties are determined by what they love, commitment to ideas and to causes is both crucial and decisive. It follows that a man's freedom to think is intimately and vitally connected with the kind of ideas and persons to which he commits himself.

HOWARD TILLMAN KUIST, *These Words Upon Thy Heart,* p. 123

5.

*The free person
accepts responsibility for
the outcome of his choices*

Once we have chosen to follow Christ, we, by virtue of our choice, fall heir to certain responsibilities, such as:

We must love—even our enemies.
We must forgive others, because God has forgiven us.
We must tell the world about God's love in Jesus Christ.
We must use our talents and share our resources.
And
We must extend personal freedom to others—
even our husbands
and wives.

St. Paul said, "For freedom Christ has set us free."

Five-point decision-making program
for daily living

1. Become informed.
2. Think about the information.
3. Come to a decision for action.
4. Perform the action.
5. Be willing to take the consequences of your action.

FR. FRANCIS EIGO

[77

A man tells things the way they are:
> "At my school women teachers have never been permitted to pray out loud at the faculty meetings. The other day some women brought this to the attention of the president who then said he'd give permission for them to lead in prayer. But so far none of the women have taken him up on the offer . . . "

Is there no one at the school who will take the consequences of the action?

> One of my firmest beliefs is that liberation does not come from the outside. Rather one is liberated through an internal process. So women will not be liberated until they decide that they want to be.
> *Participant in Conference of Women Theologians,*
> *Alverno College*

When will women decide they want to be free?

When will men be willing to free women and take the consequences of their action?

Read on.

Michael Korda contends that men in general want to keep women from becoming successful. He identifies the motive as fear.

Behind men's often petty attitude toward successful women lies the fear of women's acquiring power, both the power to live their own lives independently and the power to influence the lives of men. If women find it hard to get to the top, it is not just because men instinctively band together against the idea of a woman sharing the benefits of great success, but because the idea of a woman ordering their world from above is as unthinkable as a female Godhead.

Perhaps we recognize that power is a kind of freedom, and that what women want is the same freedom to make choices that men have. There has always been, in men, an instinctive fear that the more extreme feminists may be right, that women are in fact a more successful artifact of nature than men. The complexity of their biology, their miraculous ability to give birth to another human being, the early imprint of a mother's power on every man, all conspire to produce in men a slight feeling of awe about the potentials of women once they are unleashed. Men have trained themselves to compete, particularly in terms of power, but nothing has prepared them for competition with women, and behind their dogmatism and small guiles lies the fear that woman may in fact be a formidable competitor, once she has made her choice.

Male Chauvinism! How It Works, p. 146

I think that a woman can be liberated only if she has the support of her husband and he is not threatened by her.

ROMA WALSTROM, interview

When we are youngsters, one of the first scientific laws we learn is "for every action there is a reaction."

Example: Mix flour and water and a paste (sort of) is formed. Paste the cute puppy dog picture on the red construction paper. Fine. Isn't that nice? Hang the picture in the bedroom over the toy chest. Give it a few days, and what happens? The heat from the radiator dries out the paste and the dog separates from the paper. Too bad. Sit down and have a good cry.

An action may be the effect of one thing and the cause of another.

The action-reaction law works in social as well as scientific relationships. Consider what Barbara Sroka means when she says: *"When women change as a group, men have to change also."*

Flowers in the Mine Field

by Barbara J. Sroka

You've got a pain in your ego, you say? Who kicked you?—that "loud-mouthed radical women's libber" or that "insensitive, fat-headed sexist"?

Until a few years ago, Cupid was the only one armed in dealings between the sexes. The "love playground of life" is now a mine field. The women's issue has been worked up, over, around and through. Now it's time to comment on the devastation left in its wake.

Bitterness, hurt and resentment build easily, especially for females. Sometimes it seems the whole social system was designed without us in mind because we were born "female." And so the story of oppression goes.

For years, men have thought male dominance was right and proper (largely with female approval), and now, there's scriptural evidence and popular sentiment to the contrary. Attempts at aggressive male leadership are met with "Who do you think you are—Moses?"

When women change as a group, men have to change also. Outwardly, it's simple. In theory, we love and support each other in our growth in Christ. But inwardly, there's chaos, because the "change" invariably involves some toe-stepping.

Sometimes the situation involves more than our own egos.

Reprinted by permission from HIS, January 1975, Student Magazine of Inter-Varsity Christian Fellowship. © 1974.

A female friend of mine watched her Bible study for new Christians degenerate when a male member insisted on leading (after being convinced by an itinerant preacher that a woman should not teach). She was forced to give up leadership and, an hour before each study, they met so she could explain the lesson to him, so he could teach the others.

A controversy in a growing fellowship at a small college arose over the presidential choice. The outgoing president insisted on a male leader and chose the strongest of the males (all young Christians) to succeed himself. The female, who was the oldest and most mature in the group, faced being "de facto" president.

On the personal level the problems are just as real. Nothing so drains the soul as struggles with identity and sexuality. Then just when you've got the lid on the seething uncertainty of "Who am I?" someone insists you're all wrong because the Bible says so (in light of his or her interpretation, of course).

You're hurt. Someone just trampled on what took months and years to develop in your life. And you want to retaliate.

But, wait a minute. What will you gain with a full-scale counterattack?

"Revenge is the most worthless weapon in the world. It ruins the avenger while more firmly confirming the enemy in his wrong. It initiates an endless flight down the bottomless stairway of rancorous reprisals and ruthless retaliations," David Augsburger said in his book *The Freedom of Forgiveness.*

The Bible does provide the way out of divisive responses to difficult situations.

Three words, "I forgive you," are exasperatingly hard to say because they require a sacrifice by the person doing the forgiving.

"In forgiveness, you bear your own anger and wrath at the sin of another, voluntarily accepting responsibility for the hurt he has inflicted on you," Augsburger said.

If any person sincerely believes that Jesus is the true liberator from sin and servitude, then that person must sincerely forgive all offenses.

Forgiveness frees us to love. Vengeance loses its importance when the healing power of forgiveness is employed. When we first accepted God's forgiveness of our sins through Jesus' death, we experienced God's greatest expression of love. We were also relieved of facing God's wrath. That is our example.

The Bible had many reasons for saying, "Forgive one another, as God in Christ forgave you" (Eph. 4:32), not the least of which is our own mental and emotional health. For resentment swells and captures the mind and emotions and won't release itself or die out until it is voluntarily discarded.

Jesus said, "If you do not forgive men their trespasses, neither will your Father forgive your trespasses" (Matt. 6:15).

"I never forgive," General James Oglethorpe said to John Wesley.

"Then I hope, sir," said Wesley, "you never sin."

That doesn't mean weakly compromising on opinions and values. What we believe is truth must always be defended. But personal hurt and revenge don't have to be part of our stand for truth.

There are no easy answers to questions about leadership and authority. And to remain loving and forgiving when your mind and soul are being swept with bitterness and frustration is not easy either.

Forgiveness corrects the situations of the present, frees us from the injustices of the past, and heals us for the future. Whom do you need to forgive?

Now read what Nancy Barcus says about being set free as a woman by the Word of Christ.

[83

Male egotism and female insipidity are curses which Scripture, rightly read, would correct and obliterate. Persons may misuse and mistreat Scripture to suit other self-motivated purposes than those intended by Christ. The woman's problem does not arise from Scripture, but from a distortion or imbalance of scriptural principles. A chauvinistic regard for women arises, too, from inaccurate reading. The women mentioned in the New Testament were strong, dependable, faithful, unique in their own expressions of Christian love. Not "feminine." In their uniqueness they were created, first of all, in the image of God, and called, by name, by Him.

I am a Christian foremost, but biologically a woman. I am happy about both facts. But sometimes I feel pressured into roles and directions which disturb and oppress me. I don't want to be a man. But I don't want to be a lily either. I know better than to struggle for predominance or pre-eminence. I know that that undercuts the principle of mutuality just as badly as its opposite. I know that a woman can deprive a man of personal freedom and individuality as surely as a man can threaten a woman's. A self-destructive principle, which Ephesians 6 says is occasioned by the powers of darkness, would drive us all apart.

What we want is true community, true mutuality, true respect, of the type that Paul displays when he says to Timothy, "I call to remembrance the unfeigned faith that is in thee, which dwelt first in thy grandmother Lois, and thy mother Eunice; and I am persuaded that [is] in thee also" (2 Tim. 1:5).

It is not the Bible that has enslaved us, as some would say. It is the Word of Christ that sets us free.

NANCY B. BARCUS
"Jesus Doesn't Think I'm So Dumb"

A different kind of love story

Let me relate how a very special young man once encouraged me to exercise a very special freedom.

In my sophomore year of college I found out rather oddly how much I value one type of freedom: to initiate purposeful relationships, even with members of the opposite sex who might not be "safe."

My friend Jean Mould, who was a recent convert to Christianity, and I agreed that the Oberlin School of Theology library was a pleasant place to study. The walls were paneled in dark wood, the front had a fireplace, and rafters crossed the ceiling. On one side the windows looked down to a small quadrangle with flowering trees. The room itself seemed cloistered, and we could imagine that we followed in a long line of professional scholars. Furthermore, there we found the most fascinating people to talk with—male seminary students.

Our interest in these men was not romantic but apologetical. Personal experience with a few seminary professors who taught in the college religion department had led us to the conclusion that the entire seminary was infested with liberals who neither believed the Bible nor followed the Lord. (In those days I was quick to label and generalize.) That meant that the seminarians were being taught false doctrines, and we knew that St. Paul had pronounced "anathema" on that practice. In his Bible studies, our leader

[85

Fred had taught us how to deal with the stock intellectual arguments against Christianity. We were anxious to try out our apologetics on these men in the hope that they would see how they were being misled by their professors.

I speak for myself when I say that I had a certain arrogance to my approach. Without even bothering to find out what these students believed, I baited them and watched them bite. A typical conversation might go something like this:

> C: "I understand that Dr. ———— says Christ never claimed to be God in any Gospel but John, and, of course, no one around here accepts John as authoritative."
>
> They: "That's right. John comes pretty late."
>
> C: "How, then, do you explain the passage in Matthew where Christ said he had angels?"
>
> They: "What's that supposed to show?"
>
> C: "Well, didn't the Jews believe that angels belonged to God?"
>
> They: "We don't know. That's never come up."
>
> C: "They did. The Old Testament always speaks about angels as belonging to God. If so, how could Christ say that he would send *his* angels to cast unbelievers into punishment? *His* angels. And that's from Matthew, not John."
>
> They: "Some redactor could have added that."
>
> C: "What's your evidence for this?"
>
> They: "The early Church saw Jesus as a special person and put words into his mouth."
>
> C: "How about Jesus' claim to forgive sins? You're not going to tell me that's only in John. It's in all three Synoptics. The Jews knew only God could forgive sins, so they didn't exactly appreciate Christ's claim. Blasphemy deserved death, and they made sure he got it."

From here we might go on anywhere and often did, caught in the disorganization that characterizes most verbal sparring, talking past each other but enjoying the challenge. Jean would chime in perceptively but less aggressively. She was more for the one-to-one personal talk and probably got farther than I did. We both liked to think we were "witnessing" for Christ; possibly I was doing battle with straw men.

While these excursions into the bastion of liberalism were still going on, our Christian group had a visit from the newly appointed Inter-Varsity staff representative, a modern day Paul who checked up on the outposts of believers. Through the grapevine he had heard that Jean and I were fraternizing with seminarians. One night in front of Ellis Cottage where I lived he had a talk with me and strongly advised that we should stop. I remember his words: "Those men aren't interested in your sweet Christian testimony, Carolyn. They're men and have their minds on something else."

Although I regarded my counselor warmly, I did not want to accept his analysis of the situation. He hadn't been there; he didn't know what was taking place; and furthermore, I could take care of myself.

By this time Fred and I were firm friends. In fact, toward the end of my freshman year, our bonds had gone beyond friendship. Neither of us believed in going steady, so we were free to date others and did. Our relationship had the lapses that usually accompany such an arrangement. At the time I was dating someone else. Still I knew where I could get support.

It was Saturday night and Fred would be on duty in the snack bar. After the staff member had left me, I raced up there. "I've got to talk to you," I blurted out.

"O.K. Come on back here." Fred motioned to a room behind the counter. It was small and steamy. I knew my hair would go limp, but I stepped inside.

"I've just been told that I should have nothing to do with those men from the seminary." Fred knew Jean and I had been going over there.

"Who told you that?" he inquired.

I described what had happened and waited for his response.

"That's ridiculous!" he said, definite as usual. "You can go over there anytime you want to. I know you can handle yourself."

Fred had told me what I wanted to hear. My freedom to witness would not be restricted. The matter, then, was settled. I knew I could count on him to give me all the latitude I wanted and the vote of confidence to spur me on.

That night Fred walked me back home under the trees to Ellis Cottage.

6.
The free person has a realistic view of his strengths and weaknesses

A college student comments:
"The problem is that some people are so clever at rationalizing that they hoodwink themselves."
"On Labeling Oberlin Students"

We have been so dishonest with ourselves about ourselves for so long that we take our dishonesty to be the honest truth.

FRED KEEFE

Makeup by Satan

Satan can work wonders
with his grease paint and cotton balls.
It was clever of him
to apply base-white first. "How
interesting," I thought, "Now
I have the look of the girls
who slink down the runway
for a big price." Next
he rubbed the silken, ashen masque
over every waiting pore. I could tell
he had a deft hand,
the most practiced in the trade.
Then he arched my brows,
dark and thin, a bit too high
but unmistakably chic.
The age lines were drawn,
three or four beside my nose
and edging my eyes.
I liked the downward stroke,
a depravity I could feel
and act out, the hardness
painted in around the cheek
scar and yellowed teeth.
Finally over all he laid
a powdery set, a fine-grain matte
which will never wash off.
See—Satan has given me
a beautiful new face.

"To idealize ourselves or others can only lead to unreality," says William Yeomans.

In the business of living the starting point is always now. It is always this slightly or highly unsatisfactory situation in which I find myself. We are all people in a state of incompletion, divided in ourselves, living in a world which is also incomplete and divided. The temptation to wait until everything happens just right, has to be constantly resisted. We have to begin from what we are and from where we are. To want a perfect me in a perfect world before I begin is to want the end at the beginning. The lesson of God's love in the bible is a constant reminder that he not only can, but always does, take us as we are, and asks only one step at a time and the readiness to accept any further steps that the first one may lead to; but we must not ask for any guarantees about the nature of the second and third or the ten thousandth step.

In order to begin we have to learn to leave go, to loosen that grasp on ourselves which is the equivalent of burying our talent in the earth. But how many find themselves discontented with themselves as they are, and yet without the courage to leave go and launch out in the search? There seems to be no road out of the impasse, and yet there is. Eventually we must either choose to turn in more and more upon ourselves or to accept to share our own inadequacy with others, or rather to accept that our inadequacy is shared, that it is part of the human situation. To idealize ourselves or others can only lead to unreality. All our idols have feet of clay just because they are idols—the product of imperfect people. There can be a great deal of self-deception in the comparison of myself with others to the detriment of myself. This acceptance of a shared experience of inadequacy demands nothing short of an act of faith. To say that we all seem unequal to our task, that we are all more or less unsuccessful human beings, that we do not love as we should, that we have not got the concern we know we ought to have: to say this and then to start out, this is real faith.

WILLIAM YEOMANS, "The Starting Point"

Lessons in "astronomy"

One of the hardest lessons to learn in life is "How many and which stars can I reach?"

"Astronomy" lessons begin in early childhood when imagination is natural and charming. A gentle little boy suddenly becomes a fierce tiger who by growling and snapping his teeth is able to rule his jungle kingdom. Just behind the sofa live fire-spitting dragons. Crooks hide in the basement and spooks in the attic. Never fear, the boy has hung a ready supply of guns, swords, spears, knives, helmets, and shields where grown-ups see only the walls. Within seconds all enemies—beastly, human, and ghostly—will be dead or begging for mercy. There is nothing, absolutely nothing, that he cannot do or be.

A shy little girl suddenly becomes a stately queen with thousands of subjects—human and animal—under her control. Her mother's out-of-fashion dress falls in purple velvet folds about her feet. The cheap metal chain which she circles around her waist bears clusters of garnet blossoms and sculptured gold leaves. When she rises from her silver throne, her subjects cower beneath her glimmering scepter, a broom borrowed for "just a minute, Mommy." The Black Knight who refuses to fight in the queen's army is banished forever from the land. The bad lion who goes around biting nice little girls is warned that he must stop it or he'll be shot to death—or something worse. With great flourishes of her royal wand she transforms plastic buttons to gold pieces, and with them buys one hundred silk gowns and slippers to match. Her justice is cocky and swift, her command instantaneous and boundless.

By the time a child goes to school, if not before, she may find that others can reach a lot farther than she can. Someone is always reading faster, computing more accurately, jumping higher, drawing better, and speaking more fluently. The teacher seems to call on only a few students, and she's not one of them. She is never suggested for class committees or asked to carry notes between rooms. At bat she's always in ninth place. The days when lions shook under her scepter seem a long way back. Perhaps they never existed at all. She may conclude that the song about wishing on a star and having dreams come true is merely a Disney fable.

Being eclipsed by someone else is also the common experience of adults. No matter how rich, beautiful, intelligent, talented, or witty we may be, there are others who can beat us out in one way or another. You buy a sleek new sailboat, fifty feet of dreams come true, and as a strong, warm wind puffs out the magnificent sails, a yacht streaks by. You're glad you can't hear what is shouted from the deck, but you see the unmistakable derision on the face of a deck hand. Or at the barbershop you're telling the boys how you know all the baseball averages way back to the fifties. Then along comes your boss who can do for three sports what you can do for one. So you have to step back behind the line where most of us stand as a matter of course.

Feelings of inferiority accompany the realization that often we cannot claim "Anything you can do, I can do better." How we cope with these feelings will determine whether or not we develop into what Abraham Maslow calls "self-actualized persons." These persons are realistically oriented and accept themselves, other people, and the natural world for what they are, not for what they *wish* them to be.

They know that no one can excell in everything, or even be second best, but that every person has the responsibility to make optimum use of his native abilities, his training, and his experience.

What happens to a person who refuses to make a realistic appraisal of himself is frightening. In *What Life Should Mean to You,* Alfred Adler explains that discouragement is debilitating: the person is not able to get rid of his feeling of inferiority through constructive efforts at improving his situation, so he may feign tryannical superiority. "In this way he may drug himself; but the real feeling of inferiority will remain. They will be the same old feelings of inferiority provoked by the same old situation. They will be the lasting undercurrent of his psychic life. "

The words of Christ are even more compelling, for they have import for the psyche now and in the life to come. Jesus told his disciples about a master who before he left on a journey entrusted his property to his three servants according to their abilities. Upon returning he expected to find that each servant had wisely invested his portion, but such was not the case. One man had buried his share which unlike that of the others had not increased a whit in value. The upshot of the matter was that the wicked servant was cast into "the outer darkness; there men weep and gnash their teeth."

Obviously Christ was not talking about monetary values but of human capabilities. The "talents" ran from five to one, from superior to below average. The issue at stake, however, is not how gifted a person is but how he has used what he has received from the Master. The man with five talents netted a one hundred percent gain; likewise, the man with the three talents. The Master's response to both was identical: "Well done, good and faithful servant; you have been faithful over a little, I will set you over much; enter into the joy of your master."

Even for Christians who want to put their talents to good

use for God, the process of discovering what they are can be a hard one. We are so self-defensive of our being or what Reuel Howe calls our "ontology," and we resent the smallest challenge to our abilities, even when that challenge comes from within. It's easy to gloss over our inadequacies, if not our faults, by denying their existence or by convincing ourselves that they are not really glaring.

The honesty required of believers comes from interaction with Christ himself, from placing ourselves at the disposal of the Master. It is the Lord alone who can give us the courage to accept what we are, because what we are has already been accepted by him. Then as we continue to be used by Christ, we learn to identify our strengths and our weaknesses and become less and less defensive about ourselves.

When we no longer have to pretend to protect our being, we are freed to pretend just for the fun of it. In this way we strike a balance between reality and make-believe. We still get a kick out of wishing on a star, but we also know that discipline, not fairy dust, will work magic on our bulges and sloth.

To say that our self-concept develops as we learn to trust in Christ does not discount the effect of human beings upon our lives.

*Our self-concept grows out of a **context.***

As an individual develops and acquires skills, he thinks of himself as one who can do things, and his important people may hold a variety of expectations of him: "He's clumsy," "He never can do anything right"; or, "I can always count on him," "He's got the right stuff in him." Out of his achievements and the attitudes of others toward him, his sense of self-esteem and prestige is built, little by little. As crisis after crisis is passed and the individual meets each of them with reasonable resourcefulness and receives the encouragement and recognition of others, he begins to believe in himself, to have a consistent expectation of what he will do in the face of various circumstances and relationships. In this way he begins to acquire a style of living which is his own and which contributes to his sense of identity and to others' identification of him.

In the achievement of a sense of self-identity, the child needs models with which to identify himself. Especially is this true during his adolescence. He needs association with men who are clear about being men, and women who are clear about being women, and who are capable of and practice a reasonably wholesome relationship with each other. He needs men and women who have convictions, who can distinguish between right and wrong, who hold these convictions firmly, and yet not rigidly. He needs guides and counselors who can help him bring together and concentrate his various and fluctuating drives and interests, and who are not dismayed or misled by the inconsistencies and fluc-

tuations that may accompany his development. He needs
help in choosing a job, because self-identification is
dependent upon some kind of occupational identity.
Finally, he needs help in acquiring, as a part of his
sense of self-identity, a sense of vocation, of being called
to something that is greater than himself, which will
draw him forth as a participant in the deepest meaning
of life. The providing of this kind of relationship to help
the individual acquire an indispensable sense of identity
is [one] of love's objectives.

REUEL HOWE, *Herein Is Love*, pp. 76–77

*We experience God within a setting passed down to us—
and what happens when we do cuts out a new self!*

Revelatory experience is never separate from tradition
but is in—and over against—tradition. The Biblical
model of a person who has seen God is one who has
to re-form his self. He must re-form his self-concept in
the light of the experience he has had with God. In
Christian theology a person who has experienced Jesus
Christ as Lord and Savior has a transforming experience
which slowly brings a new self into being. This new self
is not cut out of a preconceived pattern but is formed
against the background of the tradition that nurtured
the person. Having a conversion experience shatters
one's deepest memories and dearest internal possessions
in order to rebuild one's life more consciously about a
different center and toward a different goal.

C. ELLIS NELSON, *Where Faith Begins*, p. 83

What we think we can do—
and what we think others can do—
arises out of **context.**

This picture was drawn in 1970 by an eight-year-old girl
after she had seen me preside at a meeting.

Is it likely that before the seventies a girl—or a boy—would
have conceived of possibility in this way?

[101

7.

The free person does not fear death

Man can be master of nothing while he fears death, but he who does not fear it possesses all.

LEO TOLSTOY, *War and Peace*, XI, ix

What If Death?

Must we write about death only
when we can still feel
what it is to live
lest bereft of life
we shall not have a single image
for our pens?
What if death is a Place to Be
where every code we have ever known
is but the long unused babbling
of an extinct race of men
and all who ever spoke
are taught a new tongue of praise?
What if death is a Place to Be
where a retina of light transplants
these poor myopic eyes
and the dark prism of our narrow sight
is pierced by one bright beam of God's glory?

Shortly after the death of a close friend, the Reverend Dr. Frederick Evans wrote this account.

The friend was Dr. George Wells Arms who had served pastorates in Washington, Ohio, Minnesota, and New York. His last charge was the Bedford-Central Presbyterian Church of Brooklyn, New York, where my husband became a Christian.

Dr. Arms was our dear, loving friend too. During the winter months, "Uncle George" was at our home on Sundays, and our experience with him matched that of the Evanses.

This account is not presented to magnify George Arms but to show how one man freed by Jesus Christ faced death unafraid.

George and I have been friends for well over fifty years. For the last twenty-two years we have been unusually close, for we have lived only four miles apart. During the last eight years we were privileged to have him as our dinner guest on Saturdays. His last Saturday on earth was spent with us. When we were told on Wednesday, September 9, that he had gone Home, Mrs. Evans remarked, "How different our Saturdays are to be with George not coming!"

What a preacher and teacher of the Word of God he was. How many must have been the sinners "translated out of the kingdom of darkness into the kingdom of God's dear son" through the witness of his lips and life! How many saints or believers must have been edified, or built up in their most holy faith, through his interpretation and application of the Scriptures! Toward the end more than once he expressed regret that he could no longer preach from the pulpit, and I would say, "George, you *are* preaching, witnessing through the many tracts you have written." On his very last Saturday with us he, in a note of subdued joy, said that the American

Tract Society had just informed him that they had published during 1969, as I now recall it, 128,000 of his tracts.

How priceless his fellowship in Christ, and our conversations together, centering mainly around our Lord and Savior, and the Word, and death and Heaven. Never have I known a Christian more delivered from the fear of death than George Arms, and more sure of Heaven, that surety based alone on the victories of the Lord Jesus for him on the Cross and in Joseph's lovely garden. How often he counseled me that when I prayed for him I should *not* pray that the Lord keep him here. He *so* wanted to go to his Heavenly Home where he would forever be with his Lord, and the loved ones gone on ahead, especially his dear wife, Marguerite, to whom he still felt joined.

And so it was that when I heard the news that he was gone, I lifted my eyes to Heaven and cried, "Hallelujah, Lord, George is Home where he longed to be. You have taken him Home with no eye seeing."

George Wells Arms has joined that sacred throng yonder, has fallen at his Lord's feet in humility and gratitude, has lifted up his voice in the new and everlasting song, and has crowned Him Lord of all! That is the full assurance of our Christian faith! *Amen!*

Because I live, you will live also.   John 14:19b.

Where I am, there shall my servant be also.   John 12:26b.

You have come to fulness of life in him.   Colossians 2:10a.

Death is tremendous because life is, and because in it life says its last word. Little wonder that James Denney, in protesting against the modern tendency to make light of human death, should have added that "it is the greatest thought of which we are capable, except the thought of God." The fact which is here inescapable is a dilemma. Either we despair, or we believe. There is no middle course, no razor-edge of noncommittal on which to balance precariously. Only he who believes in God wins the victory over despair. Only the infinite mercy of the Eternal Love, incarnate, suffering, dying, rising from the dead, is big enough for the tragedy of human existence. The dilemma is inescapable. Either despair which is Hell, or faith in him who giveth us the victory.

J. S. WHALE, *Christian Doctrine,* pp. 178–79

A friend who during her college years gave herself to the Lord and then introduced him to her mother, writes about an intimate experience with death:

December, 1974

On February 4th of this year, the Lord took my dear mother to be with himself. I was with her at the time.

God blessed me greatly when he gave me my mother. If he had never blessed me in any other way, I would have no cause for complaint. I will be everlastingly grateful for my dear Mom, her love, and for the fact that he kept us together for over forty-two years!

In thinking back on the oftentimes painful events during Mom's last hospitalization, I can be thankful for many things. One is that she was fully conscious and mentally alert, and we were able to communicate with each other, even after her tracheotomy. I am thankful that she did not have a second heart attack. She suffered accutely with the one she had in 1965 and was somewhat apprehensive about the possibility of having to go through another one. She never had to. I'm thankful for the skill, understanding, and kindness of Mom's doctors. Their friendship did much to sustain me during that period. But most of all, I am thankful for our Lord and Savior Jesus Christ, whom to know is Life Eternal. His presence in our lives, especially during recent years, was the difference between hope and despair. As Mom walked through "the valley of the shadow of death" last year, she did so confidently and without fear, for she knew with whom she walked. She knew he could never fail her or forsake her, and she often said so. She had proven him over and over since she had asked him to come into her heart and life in 1950. She knew him to be altogether trustworthy.

I have found him to be trustworthy, too. He was there with me as I stood helplessly by Mom's bedside, seeing her

[109

life slip away. He took the fear out of my heart and replaced it with peace. I can't explain it. I don't really understand it. But I know that by the power of his Holy Spirit he was there, flooding my heart and mind with the knowledge of his presence and his peace which passes understanding.

And he is with me now, helping me to face the lonely times, providing guidance, friends, interests, and work to do. We have a wonderful God! He alone, our Creator and Redeemer, can satisfy the longing of our human hearts! His grace *is sufficient* for our needs. Only in Him can we find "fulness of joy," in the midst of sorrow. Praise God: "He giveth songs in the night."

CLAIRE PARKER

A man has shared his thoughts on the death of an old friend—

and a woman has laid bare her heart, broken but still praising, ten months after her mother died.

Here now are my reflections on my father's death which came early in my life and gave subsequent meaning to all that has followed—

Inasmuch as physical death is a part of even the liberated life, there is no point in pretending it doesn't exist. In my own case, the reality of death confronted me early. When I was three months past my fourth birthday, I learned what happens when a father is snatched away. I am told that he was tall and handsome, built for fighting fires and tracking game, gentle with animals and little girls. Called home in the dead of winter, just as the Depression was settling in, he left a wife, two daughters, a hunting dog, and a mortgaged home.

Although my father had been sick for several years, it was not until six weeks before his death that my mother heard the diagnosis which she then relayed to him: he would never get well. Not one who easily gave in to danger or weakness, he remained active as long as he could, but finally he was forced to bed in the little room above the kitchen. My memory of his dying is a montage of a pale face and dark hair against white sheets and of voices—the muffled whispers and sobs I heard through the clothes chute that dropped to the basement from his room.

While I did not directly experience how my father who dearly loved the Lord came to a place of quiet resignation, I have heard the story many times. One day after my father had taken to bed, my uncle brought his pastor, Dr. M. R. De Haan, to visit him. Apparently Dr. De Haan sensed that my father was troubled. After all, he *was* dying and had not yet reached thirty-six years of age or seen his wife financially secure or his girls grown up. But he was God's child with a Father whose resources were without limit. Dr. De Haan reminded him of this: "Mr. Berglund, don't you think that God can care for your wife and daughters better than you can?" I don't know if my father nodded or spoke. Possibly he said nothing. Yet his affirmation wrought the miracle just when death was the cruelest, when life still intruded and seemed worthy of being grasped. Down in the kitchen I may have caught snatches of that conversation of healing. Heard or unheard it affected my life and helped prepare me for the time when I too shall have to face death.

Often I have remarked to my family that if I could choose a time to die it would be in the spring just around Easter. That is when I go out to the garden and pull up all my withered marigold plants which through the winter have looked quite natural in situ, bleak stalks matching bleak skies. But now something has happened. A forgotten tulip has surprisingly bloomed red in the midst of the winter decay. What's dead looks even deader now. It's time to root out the old and give the sun a chance to work on the new.

If the reappearance of plant growth reminds me of the promise of life after death, so much more does the reinactment of our Lord's Passion and Resurrection. In our church it begins on Maundy Thursday with the celebration of the Last Supper. On all sides of the sanctuary the stained glass windows have turned gray as though the blackness of the betrayal night has eclipsed all exterior light. But a glow comes from the candles mounted in tall brass lanterns all along the center aisle where elders bear in human hands the symbols of costly grace. The hour seems to hang between time and eternity. Across the years a Man who knows he will die tomorrow speaks about betrayal, love, joy, tribulation, forgiveness, peace, and life eternal. Then on Good Friday the daylight reveals what the shadows could not—the stark horror of the act, the stricken Christ calling out seven words from a Roman cross, the slow, six-hour bloodletting of God's own Son. For a part of three days we wait for that life to reassert himself and rekindle our own faith in his promise: "Because I live, you will live also." It happens every Easter morning just as he said it would to all those who gather in his name.

Yes, spring would be a glorious time to die when the natural world is being reborn and faith in Christ is most poignantly real.

I can honestly say that I do not fear dying. There was a period when I asked God to let me live long enough to teach my children about him. Talk of H-bombs, fallout shelters, and Cuban missiles was in the air. Often when I'd wake at night, I'd think about the terror of little children, my Cheryl and Larry, separated from their parents. I also was concerned for dogs, especially my Scotty who wouldn't eat when I was gone. I imagined and prayed and prayed and imagined. Fortunately the midnight fantasies had a way of losing themselves at dawn; the years have seen my daughter and son grow into Christian personhood; and now I look on dying more as adventure than as an abrupt end to the duties I enjoy.

Many times I have wondered what life after death will be like. In heaven will there really be streets of gold, walls of jasper, and gates of pearl? If so, will I like such opulence? (Now I dislike gaudiness.) How can my essential personality be preserved and still be purged from sin? How large will heaven have to be to avoid a population problem? Will we know all there is to know? How will we keep busy and motivated?

Don Davies, formerly a professor at Lincoln University where my husband taught for nine years, opened up my mind to some interesting possibilities for life in other worlds, if not in heaven. "Did you ever think that God may be working

in an entirely different way in different parts of the universe?"
he asked as we were seated in the study of our first manse.

"What do you mean?" I replied.

"Well, in our world the principle is grace. Christ died on
the cross for our sins, was the sacrifice acceptable to God, and
we are saved by trusting in Christ, even though in ourselves
we have no merit."

I nodded.

"In another world it might be possible to have a different
basis for relationship with him."

"Such as?"

"Maybe God wouldn't need to become incarnate at all,"
he offered. "God could reveal himself in other ways, ways
we can't even imagine."

Obviously we were trapped within the limitations of our
language system. We had no words to name experiences we
had never had, and without those experiences, we couldn't
conceive of an existence totally unlike our own. We could
only compound ideas by taking bits and pieces, the sounds
and smells, the sight and touch of what we call life. We could
end up with talking beasts and silent men, or purple grass
and green sky, but beyond that we could not go.

As yet I had not entered C. S. Lewis's Land of Narnia
where a moment of our time can be a generation or more,
and a talking Lion romps with children and loves them.
I sojourned there after my good friend Libbie Gutsche asked:
"Haven't you read the Narnia books? Then you must." With
me went Cheryl and Larry, the three of us seated on the bed,
just before lights-out. Together we read all seven chronicles,
and I cried more than they did. Since then my world has not
been the same.

The thought that in some other time and place God will
enable us to burst out of ourselves captivates me. I'd like
to be able to describe something no man has ever known. I
would start all over to write my poem about the void before

time was. Frankly, I'm stymied, because I don't have the words and making them up doesn't work. On the other hand, we may have no need for description. What if we can know anything and everything merely by intuition? What if God unshackles every sense we have until infinity itself becomes our field of experience?

Now I can only dream of ultimacy. Then I shall see Him face to face, and to do that, everything but God must change.

Rapture

Although it is still night
the eastern sky has awakened me
with her singing,
lovely chorus of nightingales
and violins and harps in perfect tune
like the music of waterfalls in springtime.
It brings to me all the sweetness
there ever was, converging
in one sharp image before my very eyes,
sun and shadow points, palpable moonlight
that lives mysteriously after sunrise,
the lilac tinted with rainbows,
your dear face lost by the years.
My beautiful Lord has come without warning,
stepped out of dawn to a single trumpet blast
    The Great Unheard
     shouted
  in one sustained word of splendor
   the focus held, gathering
    all glory to Himself
    and All into glory.

STUDY GUIDE

This study guide is suitable for discussion in the college classroom or adult church school, cell study group, women's circle, and conference. It has been designed for eight sessions, but the material is adaptable to more or fewer meetings.

Ideally, each person should have his own book so that he can read the text before the group convenes. This is essential for optimum group functioning. On-the-spot reading is discouraged, not only because it wastes discussion time but because the intended nuances of the writers will most likely be lost, and with that loss will go the personal discoveries that make learning worthwhile and compelling.

While written preparation may deepen the level of perception and enhance discussion, such homework generally should not be mandated; the participants, however, will be asked to share their experiences as they relate to the ideas and principles found in the seven sections of the book.

The group ambience which makes the desired growth possible results from certain voluntary behaviors of the members. The first is the willingness to think. Many people become visibly disturbed when the leader stops lecturing and starts questioning. "Don't put me on the spot; it's your job to tell me what you know," seems to be their attitude, as though a leader can pour in knowledge as easily as she fills a milk pitcher. It's the members' responsibility to bring their brains with their bodies. Nothing will deaden a group faster than mental absenteeism.

Another important willingness is that of sharing. The best groups are those where each member assumes an obligation for giving information and expressing feelings, for the learning experience feeds on communication exchanges. Domination by one or a few persons limits the input range, and the conclusions drawn may be lopsided, not to mention inaccurate. Keeping quiet in libraries and hospitals may be laudable but not in group discussion. An idea may seem irrelevant and silly to one "sitting" on it, especially if that person tends to deprecate himself; expressed, it may lead the group to an important insight.

A willingness to listen to the ideas of others is also vital to good group discussion. Not everyone is equally fluent, interesting, and perceptive; some people are downright dull communicators, but in a successful group, all individuals feel a sense of worth. Sometimes this is called member satisfaction, and it is related to how each person sees his contribution to the overall functioning of the group. Verbal and nonverbal reinforcement of praise, friendship, and appreciation help develop positive group feeling, and even the most hesitant and least capable person will be encouraged to express himself.

A willingness to change is an additional mark of a growing group. The fact that all learning is a change of some sort often comes as a surprise to people, until, that is, they think about the maturation of a baby. His early rapid learning is accompanied by rapid change in size, appearance, vocal sounds, muscular skills, and mental abilities. (We all fear the lack of infant change and call that severe retardation.) While the changes brought about by later learning are not nearly as spectacular as the infant's, they nevertheless do occur as modification of knowledge, attitudes, and behavior. In a group these changes come about by studying concepts and sharing experiences, ideas, and feelings, all which lead the individual to think and react and behave a bit differently. Hopefully, for the Christian these changes result in making him grow increasingly into the stature of Jesus Christ.

All this is to say that the overriding group goal should be the synthesizing of experience, as mentioned in the Preface. The participants should thoughtfully relate all the concepts found in this book, as well as the experience flowing out of the group, to their own autobiographies. And to what purpose? That they will develop into more rational, appreciative, understanding, analytical, loving, worshipful, repentant, joyful, and free creatures, not by virtue of their humanity but through the grace and mercy of God's dear Son.

Session 1. The free person faces up to what human beings are like

Page   Discussion
14   1. Genesis 1:27 tells us that God created us in his own image. What does that mean?
17   2. *Psalm 8:3–8*. What experience prompted the Psalmist to contemplate the nature of man? Share any similar experiences you may have had. What were your conclusions about God and man?
            3. Suggest adjectives that describe mankind in this passage.
            4. What does the selection say about our responsibility to the environment, including lower animals?
            5. How does the saying "There is no God" show that a person is a fool?
            6. *Psalm 14:1–3*. Suggest adjectives that describe mankind in this passage.
            7. How can you square this view with that in Psalm 8:3–8?
18   8. Karl Menninger claims that during the Nazi era many people refused to believe that Hitler's

Page	Discussion
	atrocities were taking place, even though there was ample evidence to support that claim. What present-day massive evils are we ignoring? Can anything be done about them?
18–19	9. Do you agree with Pascal that humans exert tremendous energy in hiding their faults? Explain.
	10. What faults might you be hiding? How do you respond when a person puts a finger on one of your faults?
19–20	11. Discuss Reinhold Niebuhr's statement: "Man contradicts himself within the terms of his true essence." Does seeing yourself as a contradiction help to explain your behavior?
	12. How has man's wrong use of his freedom led to his destruction?
15	13. Now go back to "God Is a Midwife" and discover these theological themes: 1) man's sinfulness, 2) God's concern for man, and 3) man's concern for man.
	14. Which part of Niebuhr's "contradiction" predominates in this poem?
	15. In what ways does the God-midwife metaphor add to your understanding of God and man?

Session 2. *The free person is able to make choices—I*

23	1. If we follow C. S. Lewis's argument, are we justified in saying that were we not free to be bad, goodness would not have any virtue? Explain.
24	2. Can you think of any biblical characters who like the fetus in "Choose Dark" seemed not to choose light? Has your experience ever matched theirs?
25–26	3. Do you agree with Virginia Mollenkott's analysis of Proverbs 3:5–6? Have you ever used this approach in decision making? If you feel so inclined, share your experience with the group.
27	4. Explain why freedom eluded the girl in "Seeker Lost."
28–29	5. Which excerpt best explains your beliefs about

Page	Discussion

free will and determinism? Do you totally disagree
with any of the authors?

30–32   6. Which cartoon character do you think best
understands the Bible on this subject? Explain your
answer.

33   7. Explain how the hymn "I Sought the Lord" sup-
ports the particular position expressed by the character
on page 32. If conditions are right, you might want to
sing the hymn you have just studied.

NOTE: Before you disband for this session, assign reading parts
for "The Temptation of Mary" which will be used in the next
session. Do not let the idea of a dramatic reading intimidate you;
a person does not have to be an actor to read a part. Scenery,
costumes, lighting, and movement are not needed. So don't miss
the enjoyment of a play reading, followed by discussion.

Session 3. The free person is able to make choices—II

35–44   After the presentation of "The Temptation of Mary,"
discuss these questions:

1. Do you think that it is natural for a woman
who has just given birth to wonder about her child's
future? Share your feelings and experiences.

2. What temptation do each of the visitors repre-
sent? Why is each morally dangerous?

3. Find parallels between Mary's temptation and
that of Jesus. (See Luke 4:1–12.)

4. C. S. Lewis has said, "To love at all is to be
vulnerable. Love anything, and your heart will certainly be wrung and possibly be broken. If you want
to make sure of keeping it intact, you must give your
heart to no one, not even to an animal. Wrap it carefully round with hobbies and little luxuries; avoid all
entanglements; lock it up safe in the casket or coffin
of your selfishness. But in that casket—safe, dark, mo-
tionless, airless—it will change. It will not be broken;
it will become unbreakable, impenetrable, irredeem-
able" (*The Four Loves*, p. 169). Discuss how this

[123

might have applied to Mary in her love for Jesus, had she taken a selfish approach. You may want to share some of your own personal understandings of Lewis's words.

Session 4. The free person accepts god's grace

48–52   1. What are the minimum essentials for a religious experience to be called "Christian"? Talk about whether or not you think the religious experience of each man (Hammarskjöld, Finney, and Hatfield) is authentically Christian. Which experience most closely resembles your own?

52   2. Discuss your understandings of Christian faith as "simply a way of being alive that no non-Christian can understand."

53–55   3. Discuss how each woman's faith experience (that of Margaret Rogers, Becky Talley, and Delena Walker) reinforces what you have discovered in your own life. Then talk about the new insights Margaret, Becky, and Delena have given you.

56–57   4. List the reasons why people give gifts. Now list the reasons why God gave us the gift of Jesus Christ. Note the contrasts and comparisons between the two lists.

5. How is God's giving related to what Tournier calls "the imperishable fellowship of God"? Is there anything comparable on the human level?

58   6. How does the poem "The Cross Is a Magnet" use the idea "Unless you turn and become like little children, you will never enter the kingdom of God" (Matt. 18:3)?

59   7. Discuss how freedom, choice, and grace were related in Augustine's life. Share how they are related in your own life.

8. Also note how grace-as-gift and grace-as-magnet are found in this passage.

Session 5. The free person knows what he values

Page | Discussion

63–67   1. Recall some of your recent decisions and try to figure out the bases for your deciding. How might different bases have affected the outcome of these decisions?

     2. How do you think the teenage clerks should have handled their wage problems?

68–71   3. Virginia Stieb-Hales says, "There may be a gap between what we say is important and what we do about it." On the left side of a paper or blackboard, list some of the things you frequently say are important to you. On the right side list the actions (and frequency of same) you have taken to implement the verbalizations. Further examine the list by trying to apply the seven criteria for a value. How many of your "talking points" are genuine values? If your list is radically depleted, keep looking in your life for genuine values, i.e., those which will meet the seven criteria.

72–73   4. In the poem "A Quality of Dreams" the old woman is being criticized for her memories and imagination which she feels add value to her life. With whom do you agree—the woman or her detractor?

     5. How does a person maintain a healthy balance between "living on memories" and "living only for today"?

74   6. Think carefully about Howard Tillman Kuist's statement as it relates to your list (question 3) and to your life in general.

Session 6. The free person accepts responsibility for the outcome of his choices

77   1. Refer to point 5 of Fr. Francis Eigo's decision-making program. Identify a consequence you are especially perturbed or bitter about. See if you can deal with that feeling. Have you failed to follow steps

Page	Discussion

1–4? Have you bypassed your understandings of grace-as-gift and forgiveness? How can your attitude toward the consequence be improved?

79 2. In paragraph 1 note the double-barreled male fear cited by Michael Korda. Do you agree with him? Explain your position. Do you agree with his over-all analysis?

3. In your own spheres of living, mention some choices which men have but women do not. Are any changes necessary or desirable? If so, how can you attempt to bring about these changes?

80 4. In what ways can a husband liberate his wife?

81–83 5. Discuss the "toe-stepping" you are experiencing in changing male-female relationships. Paraphrase what Barbara Sroka says about love and forgiveness for this "toe-stepping." Do you agree with her approach to handling resentment?

84 6. Nancy Barcus claims, "A woman can deprive a man of personal freedom and individuality as surely as a man can threaten a woman's." Explain your reasons for agreeing or disagreeing with her.

7. What are some constructive ways to achieve "true mutuality"? Here be careful not to generalize but to mention specific behaviors.

85–88 8. Personal freedom comes in many shapes and forms which are related to an individual's needs and goals. What particular needs do you think I had that were threatened by the advice that I not go to the seminary library?

9. What particular needs do you have that are not being satisfied because someone is not granting you personal freedom? Is there anything sensibly Christian you can do to gain this freedom? How can you yourself give a needed freedom to someone?

10. Is awareness of one's needs incompatible with freely giving oneself to Christ? Where do the dangers lie in each of these attitudes: 1) "I must be a fully realized person," and 2) "I have relinquished all my needs and desires for the sake of Christ"?

Session 7. The free person has a realistic view of his strengths and weaknesses

Page	Discussion
90–91	1. Probe a bit, even though it hurts: How have you been dishonest with yourself about yourself? How have you rationalized your failures?
92	2. What is the main point of "Makeup by Satan"? Do you agree with it?
	3. How does this poem reinforce your understandings of section 1: "The free person faces up to what man is like?"
93–94	4. Do you agree with Yeomans that "we are all people in a state of incompletion, divided in ourselves, living in a world which is also incomplete and divided"? Explain your answer.
	5. What does it mean that God takes us as we are?
	6. How do we bury our talents in the earth? Why do we do it?
	7. How does idealizing ourselves or others lead to unreality? Why is comparing ourselves to others detrimental to us individually?
	8. Do you agree with the last sentence description of "real faith"? Explain your reply.
95–98	9. Give some concrete examples (other than those in the book) of how a person develops feelings of inferiority and also of superiority. How can parents help their children to achieve realistic self-images? How is grace-as-gift related to your self-image?
99–100	10. Describe the profiles of a father and a mother who in your opinion would provide the role models needed by children to help them grow up into Christian personhood in today's world.
101	11. In what ways have your self and your self-concept been re-formed by your experience with God? Have these re-formings changed your goals?

Session 8. The free person does not fear death

106–7	1. What do you think were values for George Wells Arms?

2. Why do people fear death? Why was not Dr. Arms afraid to die?

108   3. Assume for a few minutes that you are not a Christian. Make a list of the things about your life that would cause you to despair. Now go over that list and discuss how Christian faith turns these despairs into victory.

109–110   4. Discuss how Claire Parker's attitude toward her mother's death are unmistakably Christian. See if you can cite Scriptural admonitions for these Christian behaviors.

111–15   5. Discuss your earliest experiences with death and how they shaped your youthful attitudes. How have your understandings changed as you have grown in your faith?

6. What questions do you have about life after death?

7. Discuss how particular books (including the Bible), music, and visual art forms have helped in your thinking about death and heaven.

8. In what ways does the fear of death shackle the life of a person?

As a closing to your study together you might want to use the following oral reading:

Alive in Jesus Christ

Three readers sit behind a table which is covered with a pastel cloth. A well-designed flower arrangement and a candle or two add to the setting. A fourth person sits behind a screen or inconspicuously to the side of the group. His job is to run a two-minute tape of appropriate classical music (Cesar Franck's Symphony in D Minor works well) or a favorite hymn. As soon as the music stops, the readers stand in unison behind the table and proceed with the reading. Slides or mounted pictures should be shown during the reading, the timing and placement being dictated by the number and subject matter of the available visuals. Readers are cautioned not to rush through the words; give the audience sufficient time to react to the sounds and sights. After the "Amen and amen," the three readers sit in unison and a triumphant selection is played on the tape recorder. The entire program should be presented with dignity and reverence, with each person knowing exactly what to do and when to do it.

Voice 1: And God saw everything that he had made, and behold, it was very good.

Voice 2: Then there was a hand stretched out—
and another,
the taking of forbidden fruit,
mouths full of sweetness turned bitter.
And God said,

Voice 1: "Because you have done this, cursed is the ground because of you; in the sweat of your face you shall eat bread till you return to the ground, for out of it you were taken; you are dust, and to dust you shall return."

Voice 2: Death comes. It comes to all:
the young lady holding a spring bouquet
the wistful girl with jam on her face
the tribesman decked out for festival
the old woman already lost in despair

Voice 1: to the sick
the vibrant
the young
the powerful
the rich
the poor

Voices 1 and 2: Death comes to all.

Voice 2: Before it came to Jesus, he said to his friends,
"Let not your hearts be troubled; believe in God, believe also in me. I am the resurrection and the life; he who believes in me, though he die, yet shall he live, and whoever lives and believes in me shall never die. In my Father's house are many rooms; if it were not so, would I have told you that I go to prepare a place for you? And when I go and prepare a place for you, I will come again and will take you to myself, that where I am you may be also."

[129

Voice 1: Jesus showed us that death does not *have* to come fearfully—
not for us who trust in the Father.
Voice 2: Possibly dying is something like—
seeing the universe in a new way,
not from the gully but from the mountain top,
Voice 1: being wrapped in sunsets which do not fade,
having senses more alive than we could ever imagine.
Voice 3: (Read "What If Death?" on p. 105.)
Voice 2: Possibly death is something like—
Voice 1: going home in the twilight after a long day's labor,
Voice 2: and seeing our blessed Lord face to face,
Voices 1 and 2: and knowing his presence and love forevermore.
Voice 3: (Read "Rapture" on p. 117.)
Voice 1: Death comes to all—
Voice 2: but not fearfully to those who are now alive in Jesus Christ.
Voices 1, 2, and 3: Amen and amen.

BIBLIOGRAPHY

"A Letter to Her Mother." *Israel for Christ,* Autumn 1964.

Aquinas, Thomas. *The Summa Theologica.* Translated by Fathers of the English Dominican Province. New York: Benziger Brothers, Inc. Vol. 19 of *Great Books of the Western World,* edited by Robert Maynard Hutchins.

Augustine, Saint. *The Confessions.* Translated by Edward Bouverie Pusey. In vol. 18 of *Great Books of the Western World,* edited by Robert Maynard Hutchins.

Baillie, D. M. *God Was in Christ.* New York: Charles Scribner's Sons, 1948.

Barcus, Nancy B. "Jesus Doesn't Think I'm Dumb." *Eternity,* February 1974, pp. 17–19.

Bloom, Benjamin, ed. *Taxonomy of Educational Objectives.* Handbook I: *Cognitive Domain.* New York: David McKay, 1956.

Conference of Women Theologians. Transcript of Opening Session, June 7-18, 1971, Milwaukee: Alverno College.

Descartes, René. *Objections against the Meditations, and Replies.* Translated by Elizabeth S. Haldane and G. R. T. Ross. Cambridge: University Press. In vol. 31 of *Great Books of the Western World,* edited by Robert Maynard Hutchins.

Eigo, Francis. "Key Issues in Spirituality." Notes on classroom lectures taken by Carolyn Keefe. Villanova, PA: Villanova University, Summer 1973.

Finney, Charles G. *Memoirs.* New York: Fleming H. Revell, 1876.

Hammarskjöld, Dag. *Markings.* Translated by Leif Sjöberg and W. H. Auden. New York: Alfred A. Knopf, 1964.

Hatfield, Mark O. *Conflict and Conscience.* Waco, TX: Word Books, 1971.

Hobbes, Thomas. *Leviathan.* Edited by Nelle Fuller. In vol. 23 of *Great Books of the Western World,* edited by Robert Maynard Hutchins.

Howe, Reuel L. *Herein Is Love*. Valley Forge, PA: The Judson Press, 1961.

Hutchins, Robert Maynard, ed. *Great Books of the Western World*. 54 vols. Chicago: Encyclopaedia Britannica, Inc., 1952.

Korda, Michael. *Male Chauvinism! How It Works*. New York: Random House, 1973.

Kuist, Howard Tillman. *These Words Upon Thy Heart*. Richmond, VA: John Knox Press, 1947.

C. S. Lewis. *The Four Loves*. New York: Harcourt, Brace & World, 1960.

————. *Mere Christianity*. New York: Macmillan Publishing Co., 1960.

————. *Surprised by Joy*. New York: Harcourt, Brace & Co., 1955.

Mead, Frank S., ed. *The Encyclopedia of Religious Quotations*. Westwood, NJ: Fleming H. Revell, 1965.

Menninger, Karl. *Whatever Became of Sin?* New York: Hawthorn Books, 1973.

Mollenkott, Virginia. *In Search of Balance*. Waco, TX: Word Books, 1969.

Nelson, G. Ellis. *Where Faith Begins*. Richmond, VA: John Knox Press, 1967.

Niebuhr, Reinhold. *The Nature and Destiny of Man*. New York: Charles Scribner's Sons, 1953.

"On Labeling Oberlin Students." *Oberlin Alumni Magazine*, November-December 1974, pp. 2–4.

Pascal, Blaise. *Pensées*. Translated by W. F. Trotter. New York: E. P. Dutton & Co., Everyman's Library. In vol. 33 of *Great Books of the Western World*, edited by Robert Maynard Hutchins.

Spinoza, Baruch. *Ethics*. Translated by W. H. White. Revised by A. H. Stirling. New York: Oxford University Press. In vol. 31 of *Great Books of the Western World*, edited by Robert Maynard Hutchins.

Sroka, Barbara J. "Flowers in the Mine Field." *HIS*, January 1975.

Stieb-Hales, Virginia. "A Process of Clarifying Values." *Concern*, July-August 1973, pp. 7–8.

Tolstoy, Leo. *War and Peace*. New York: Oxford University Press. Translated by Louise and Aylmer Maude. Vol. 51 of *Great Books of the Western World*, edited by Robert Maynard Hutchins.

Tournier, Paul. *The Meaning of Gifts*. Translated by John S. Gilmour. Richmond, VA: John Knox Press, 1963.

Whale, J. S. *Christian Doctrine*. New York: Cambridge University Press, 1952.

Yeomans, William. "The Starting Point." *The Way*, January 1970, pp. 3–9.